Rugby:

Skills, Training and Tactics

Rugby:

Skills, Training and Tactics

LES WILLIAMS

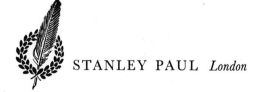

STANLEY PAUL *London*

STANLEY PAUL
178-202 Great Portland Street, London, W.1

AN IMPRINT OF THE HUTCHINSON GROUP

London Melbourne Sydney
Auckland Bombay Toronto
Johannesburg New York

First published 1962

*This book has been set in Baskerville type face. It
has been printed by offset in Great Britain by
William Clowes and Sons, Limited, London and
Beccles, on smooth white litho paper and bound by them*

Contents

Illustrations

KEY TO MOVEMENTS IN DIAGRAMS

×	attackers
○	defenders
———→—	path of ball
————→	path of runner with ball
- - - - - -→	path of runner without ball

Acknowledgements

I wish to express my grateful and sincere thanks to my friends J. B. G. (Bryn) Thomas, Sports Editor of the *Western Mail*, for his help and encouragement, Eric R. James M.A. Senior English Master, Falmouth Grammar School for his help with the script. Also to The *Western Mail* for supplying the photographs.

1 / The Elements of Rugby

STAMINA, speed, strength, agility, skill in the basic arts—and tactical ability—these are the basic demands made on rugby players. They are tangible and teachable components of the game, the basic practices of which could be introduced to boys of a very young age.

There is, of course, another aspect of the game which is far less tangible than the physical elements yet it is as significant as any of them. It is that special mental ability to learn rugby skills and tactics quickly with very little or no effort. It includes that seemingly innate knowledge of what to do when faced with rugby situations and the ability, more often than not, to do the right thing at the right time. It probably includes the natural ability to concentrate on the intended manœuvre regardless of the difficulties, whether it be in learning a skill or playing the game.

Players who possess a high degree of aptitude are the 'naturals', who have only to be shown a skill or tactic once or twice and they 'have it'. They become good at an early age and if properly nurtured they will advance into greatness. Young players who show much less aptitude may also become great, but they achieve it after much more conscious effort and practice. Learning rugby does not come easy to them, the potential is there but it takes longer to develop and mature. The 'naturals' have to practise too, of course, but they seem to have the ability to learn much quicker than the majority.

The mental element of rugby also includes attitudes of mind like courage, self-discipline, unselfishness, and sportsmanship. One does not have to be a great player to possess them but it is desirable that all players have such qualities. They do not easily lend themselves to systematic coaching, like skills and tactics, but may develop along with the process of learning the game and can be further developed by encouragement and understanding of the problems by the coach. To develop them along with the physical elements of rugby demands from the coach considerable thought and analysis of the game and skilful and patient coaching. Players must be watched not only for technical faults but also for failings in mental attitudes. Some may, at times, display poor sportsmanship or give up too easily, or throw a great burden upon the rest of the team by some selfish acts in games or in training, or lack sufficient courage and self-confidence in the play. The good coach will be aware of these faults and the need to remedy them.

A typical problem is to encourage a rather diffident, but otherwise skilful player to use his talent in a more aggressive and forceful way. Rugby is a 'man's game' and there is room in it for clean robustness and vigour. Robustness cannot be taught, but the quiet player can be encouraged to develop and use it. It would be a great mistake to let him continue playing with this fault when all that is needed is for him to experience success in this type of play. This success must be provided for him by the coach. He must be placed in artificial situations, simple at first, but gradually getting more difficult which will demand from him determination and courage of progressively increasing intensity until he becomes more forceful. A different problem is the player who abounds in energy and courage and will not cease to attack until overpowered by sheer weight of numbers. He needs to learn to be an effective link. Once in possession of the ball he forgets the rest of the team. He has not learned the art of teamwork and co-operation which can save himself and the team a good deal of wasted energy.

To encourage a young full-back to concentrate his attention on catching a high ball, and not allow himself to be distracted by the oncoming attackers, is another problem. His confidence and self-discipline need developing. Again progressive practices must be introduced, placing the player in progressively more complex situations, which as nearly as possible simulate game conditions, until the final movement can be performed no matter what the distractions.

These are not easy problems to tackle yet the way in which the game is taught in the beginning will have an important effect on the mental attitude of the players and the coach is responsible for preventing the development of fear and self-regard and, for the introduction of practices which will overcome any lack of confidence which might already be present. Success gives the players a feeling of confidence; so early practices must be within the capabilities of the players. Careful but not too slow progressions from these to more difficult skills will lead to success and self-assurance.

2/*Passing and Catching*

PASSING and catching are probably the most important of the fundamental skills, because, in the main, the quality of rugby games depends on the handling ability of the players. In fact one could almost say that rugby itself is passing and catching. These two skills more than anything else need practice and practice and still more practice, and this from an early age and continued right to the very end of the player's career.

Once the mechanics of the pass have been mastered the emphasis all the time should then be on speed, accuracy, and timing.

Being able to pass the ball far and fast does not necessarily mean being a good passer, though it helps. Passing must of necessity vary according to the many situations, and a good passer must be able to meet each situation with the appropriate type of pass. A particular situation might require a short lobbed pass, or a long lobbed pass, or a quick snappy pass, or a long low pass, or any type of pass in between the two extremes. All types must be practised if players are to reach a high standard.

To expect every pass to be perfect is perhaps asking too much, so one must be prepared for a few mistimed and misdirected passes during the course of a game, in which case catching must reach as high a standard as the

passing. By and large passing and catching will be practised simultaneously, and in order to keep the passing
practices moving continuously every effort should be
made to catch even the very bad as well as the good
passes. But for the fact that most of the better players
can catch the poor passes almost as well as they can
catch the good ones, the standard of rugby would be
much lower.

A wet ball is often looked upon as a genuine excuse
for the atrocious handling which is usually seen when
games are played in poor conditions. Certainly a wet
ball is not as easy to handle as a dry one, but when one
considers that rugby is a winter game and that it can
be assumed that about half the games are going to be
played with a wet ball, one wonders why so little
attention is given to handling practices with these
conditions in mind. A wet ball is not a genuine excuse
for poor handling; the trouble is the lack of ability to
handle a wet ball.

There is no modern or secret way to better handling,
it is purely a matter of practice, concentration, and
eyes on the target in passing, and on the ball in catching. Nine times out of ten the reason for a dropped pass
is that the receiver lacked the concentration to keep
his eyes on the ball until it was safely in his hands.
Whenever possible, both hands, with fingers well
spread, should be used when catching, unless, of course,
the pass is so mistimed that it is likely that the receiver
will overrun the ball and lose possession, and to reach
and scoop it into the body with one hand seems the
only solution. The latter is a highly skilled way of col-
lecting the ball and since it is sometimes necessary to use

this method it should be practised to perfection. But it should be used *only* when the ball cannot possibly be taken with both hands.

Emphasis on more and more speed and accuracy in passing practices will demand greater concentration from the players, and if this concentration can become second nature then handling generally is going to be better.

Holding the Ball

Ideally, the ball should be held for a pass with the fingers comfortably spread and pointing along the seams. Given time, no matter how awkwardly the ball may be received, it can always be adjusted to the correct position. There will, however, be many occasions when the passer cannot afford the time to adjust the ball, and he must pass in the next convenient stride even if the ball is held by the points to avoid being tackled in possession. Players must become accustomed to this faster type of pass by omitting adjusting the ball before the pass in many of the practices, and they must concentrate on getting rid of the ball almost as soon as it is caught.

Orthodox Pass

Under normal circumstances four strides are taken to complete the sequence of movements involved in catching and passing. For a pass to the left, if the ball is caught as the right leg moves forward to complete the first stride, during the second stride the ball is brought under full control, adjusted and is ready to be taken to a point to the right of the body. In the third stride the

16

ball is taken to the furthest right position, the left arm is across, and close to the body, the right arm is well bent and away from the side with the elbow almost level with the shoulder, the head is turned to the receiver with the eyes on the 'target', the right foot comes to the ground pointing about 45 degrees inward. As the third stride ends the delivery begins, the arms swing across to the left, over the left leg as it moves forward in the fourth stride, and are straightened with a flick of the wrists and fingers as the ball is delivered. The shoulders turn to the left with the arm swing so that the chest is almost fully open to the receiver; the left leg is carried forward and across the right leg, so that the balance lost during the delivery can be restored.

It is, in fact, possible to catch and pass in only two strides, but probably not when travelling at high speed and only when catching coincides with the correct stride. Assuming again that for a pass to the left the ball is caught as the right leg moves forward in the first stride. This is the correct stride, but instead of catching the ball in front of the body, the player must now reach to catch it at a point away to the right of the body roughly where he would normally take the ball if the pass was given at leisure, and without delay directs it to the receiver with one sweep of the arms and body as the left leg moves forward in the second stride.

Reverse Pass

The reverse pass is normally used in conjunction with a 'scissors' movement to change the direction of attack. It is a two-handed backward pass under the

2

arm. The body weight should be on the opposite foot and the head turned to look over the shoulder at the 'target'. The pass is given under the arm on the side from which the receiver comes. If he runs from the passer's right across behind him to the left, then the pass must be under the right arm. This will ensure that the receiver sees the ball all the time; whereas if the pass is made on the other side, there is a fraction of time when the ball is out of the receiver's sight. The two-handed pass is more reliable than the one-handed lobbed pass, and with it the reverse pass dummy could be attempted.

The scrum-half should use the reverse pass under the arm furthest away from the scrum, with the foot nearest the scrum forward and supporting the body weight.

Learning the Orthodox Pass—the Three-step Method

Passing to the left from standing.

1. The left foot moves forward and the head begins to turn toward the receiver.

2. Right foot forward and placed at an angle of about 45 degrees inward. The ball is taken to the furthest right position with the right elbow well bent and almost level with the shoulder. Eyes on the receiver.

3. Left foot forward and across to the right. The pass is made over the left leg. Arms are comfortably extended and the chest open to the receiver.

The Step Away

This is used to carry the body away from the direction of the pass.

The quickest way to develop the step away is to run diagonally forward and to the right and pass to the left. Providing that the pass is made off the correct foot, in this case the right, the loss of balance resulting from the vigorous twist to the left of the upper part of the body will automatically compel the passer to carry the left leg across to the right to restore balance; several practices with this method to both sides will give the passer an adequate 'feeling' for the step away.

Learning the Reverse Pass—Two-step Method

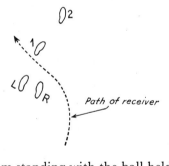

Path of receiver

Passing from standing with the ball held in front to a receiver crossing from right to left.

1. Left foot forward and turned in very slightly, the head turns to look over the right shoulder and the ball is carried forward away from the body with the elbows slightly bent.

2. The pass is delivered under the right arm as the right leg moves forward into stride two.

Turning or Swing Pass

Another form of pass which could be used in the 'scissors' movement is the turning or swinging pass. To do this the passer swings round during the run to face the receiver and gives a short lobbed pass as their paths cross. The turn should be in the direction from which the receiver comes, i.e. to the right if the receiver runs from right to left.

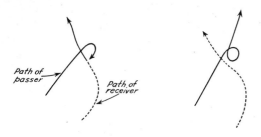

In the 'dummy' pass the player in possession retains the ball and continues the turn until he is again facing and running in the general direction of the original path. This is used when the opponents have clearly anticipated the 'scissors' but not as easy to execute as the reverse pass dummy.

Passing from the Ground

Every player will find it necessary from time to time to pass quickly and accurately from the ground but the main consideration here will be given to the four types of passes used by scrum-halves. Speed and correctness

A good example of a dive pass

ive pass. The ball is about to be passed as the feet leave the ground after
ie leg drive. Welsh wing-forward Morgan breaks from the scrum and
eads in the direction of the intended receiver

of footwork is essential to get the full effect from the leg, body, and arm drive in the pass.

The Straight Pass

This is the orthodox pass from the ground, and is used when the scrum-half intends to pass to the open side after putting the ball in on the blind side, or vice versa. For a pass to the left he will move round to face the scrum and place his right foot near and to the right of the ball with the other foot placed well away to the left and pointing roughly in the direction of the pass. The pass begins the moment the ball is picked up, and is swung straight from the ground to the receiver. The right leg drives to add momentum to the pass. There is no preliminary 'winding up', although there may be a slight bending at the elbows as the ball leaves the ground. The wide position of the left foot ensures that the passer remains on his feet after the pass. Reversed procedure applies for a pass to the right.

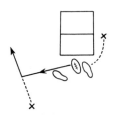

The Swing Pass

This is used when the scrum-half intends to pass to the same side of the scrum as that on which he stands, e.g. to the open side after putting the ball in on that side of the scrum. For a pass to the left he will move round to place the left foot alongside the ball and between it and the scrum. The right foot will be roughly in line but well behind the left, and turned outward (to the right) a little. At this time the scrum-half will be facing the blind side touch-line with his left arm nearest the scrum. The ball is picked up and swung clockwise to the scrum-half's right and passed to the receiver in one continuous movement. The left leg drives, and the body weight will pass over the right leg during the follow-through. The passer is likely to overbalance and fall if the right foot has been brought up too close to the left in the initial stance. The procedure is reversed for a pass to the right of the scrum, i.e. right foot near the ball with the left foot behind, and the passer swings anti-clockwise to his left to pass.

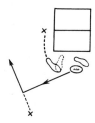

The Reverse Pass

This is the alternative to the swing pass. The conditions of passing and footwork are the same as in the

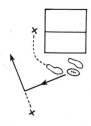

swing pass but the weight of the body moves forward over the front foot and away from the direction of the receiver in the reverse. For a pass to the left of the scrum the ball is passed under the right arm.

Pass to the left.

The Dive Pass

The purpose of the dive is to add greater momentum to the ball. Many scrum-halves appear to be using the dive pass when in fact they are usually demonstrating the simple art of falling over because of incorrect footwork in a straight pass, made with the feet too close together. For the dive pass both legs drive to impart momentum to the ball, whereas in the straight pass only the leg nearest the ball imparts drive of any consequence.

The ball should be picked up from in front of, and fairly close to the feet (often one foot may be nearer to the ball than the other) and as the legs drive the body over the ball the arms swing the ball forward and away toward the receiver. The important thing to remember about this pass is that the drive ends when the feet leave the ground, and to get the best effect from it the delivery should coincide with the end of the drive. Momentum is at its greatest at this time. The dive through the air is superfluous; it is merely the follow through of the leg drive and arm swing. To retain the ball until the body is in the air and then pass is a waste of energy and time, the pass will have been delayed and only the arm swing will give momentum to the ball.

This pass should be used only on occasions since its use puts the scrum-half temporarily out of the game.

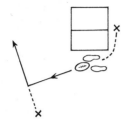

Catching a High Ball

Judgement of distance and speed of flight is important. If at all possible the ball should be caught on the full volley, that is, before it bounces. It is always better to slightly over-estimate than under-estimate the bistance of flight for it is easier to move forward at the last moment than have to stop and retreat hurriedly to get into position to catch.

The catcher should assume a well balanced stance with one foot in advance of the other; most players will place the left foot forward. The hands should be level with the face, with the fingers well spread, the elbows will be forward of the chest but pressed inward toward each other; eyes on the ball. As the ball enters this cradle the hands close inward over it and the elbows are pulled even closer together as they move down on to the lower part of the chest. The knees should 'give' a little, to minimize the force of impact as the ball comes in contact with the chest. Should the catcher misjudge the ball's flight in such a way that its descent will be slightly to his right or left, or just behind him, he must follow the ball by turning to face whichever direction the ball is likely to fall and, if necessary, step forward in the new direction to catch. Quick and correct footwork will often eliminate the chances of misfielding an awkwardly flighted ball.

Passing and Catching Practices

Stationary Passing—Most of the players are stationary during the practices.

1. *Circle Passing*—Players are arranged in circles of six facing inward. A ball is passed quickly from player to player round the circle. To speed up the passing, the number of balls should be increased until five are being passed at a time, that is, one less than the number of players making the circle.

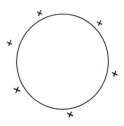

2. *Circle Passing*—Facing outward. Progress as above to five balls.

3. *Corner Spry*—(*a*) One ball. Groups of six. Nos. 2–6

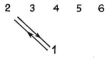

stand in a line with No. 1 out in front with a ball. No. 1 passes to No. 2, who passes it back to No. 1, and so on through the team to No. 6. No. 1 then runs to stand next to No. 2, and No. 6 takes his place in front. This continues until No. 1 returns to his place in front of the team.

(*b*) Two balls. In this variation Nos. 1 and 2 have a ball each. No. 1 passes to No. 3 as No. 2 passes to No. 1. No. 1 then passes to No. 4 while No. 3 passes back to No. 1, and so on till No. 6 and No. 1 have a ball each.

No. 6 then runs out to the front and No. 1 moves to stand next to No. 2. The procedure is repeated, No. 6 passes to No. 2 as No. 1 passes to No. 6, etc., until No. 1 returns to his place as leader.

(*c*) Two balls. Players arranged as in the diagram; Nos. 1 and 3 have a ball each. As in (*b*), both balls are passed simultaneously by two players. No. 1 passes to No. 3 as No. 3 passes to No. 4. No. 3 now passes to No. 2 while No. 4 passes to No. 1. No. 1 passes to No. 3 as No. 2 passes to No. 1, and so on.

4. *Circle Spry*—As for Corner Spry (*a*) and (*b*) but the players form a circle with the leader No. 1 holding the ball in the middle.

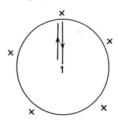

5. *Wandering Ball*—(*a*) Players arranged in circles of five with No. 1 in the centre. The ball is passed round the circle while the player in the middle tries to intercept. When he gains possession the last passer takes his place in the centre of the circle. Variations. Players change with interceptor if they were the last to handle before the ball is touched in flight; the ball is touched when in their possession; the player is touched when in possession; a player fails to catch a good pass; or if a player throws a bad pass (below knees and above shoulders).

(*b*) Players arranged in larger circles of six or eight numbered off in pairs 1 and 2, 3 and 4, etc., with two

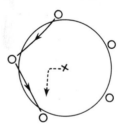

in the centre. The ball is passed around the circle while the players in the centre try to intercept. If they succeed they pass the ball among themselves inside the circle. Meanwhile Nos. 1 and 2 run into the centre to try to retrieve the ball. When they do so they return to their places in the circle and the play continues. Next time the centre players intercept, Nos. 3 and 4 enter the circle to regain the ball and so on.

6. *Tower Ball*—Five players arranged round a circle with No. 1 in the centre to guard the 'tower'. The players round the circle try to knock down the 'tower' with the ball. No. 1 may use hands, body, and legs to defend the 'tower'. Players must pass quickly to those who are in a better position to knock down the 'tower' or use the 'dummy' pass to trick the defender. The player successful in hitting the 'tower' changes with the one in the centre. 'Tower' could be a skittle, medicine ball, high jump stand, or a cricket stump, etc.

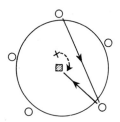

7. *Circle Passing v. Runner*—Team of six arranged in a circle with No. 1 holding the ball. The ball is passed round the circle from No. 1 to No. 2, and so on. Immediately after passing to No. 2, No. 1 sprints round the circle and tries to get 'home' before the ball. If he fails, the ball is passed direct from No. 6 to No. 2 who is the next runner. The game is continuous and the ball should not be delayed until the runner arrives back in his place.

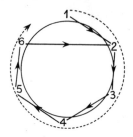

An alternative is to run outward to touch a marker instead of round the circle. The marker—sweater or handkerchief, etc., should be far enough to make the runner sprint at top speed in order to get back in time, or it may be placed much nearer and the player runs back and forth to touch it a given number of times.

Passing on the Move

1. *Running, Passing in twos*—(*a*) Emphasis on accuracy and correct footwork. (*b*) Step away at target, post, etc. (*c*) Dummy with step away.

2. *Running and Passing in Fours*—Players run and pass in a line of four. Emphasis should be on speed passing. The greatest number of passes in a set distance.

3. *Running and Passing in Fours*—Receiver accelerates for 15–20 yards and then passes and the next player accelerates and so on.

4. *Making the Extra Man Practice*—(*a*) Players run and pass in a line of four, but immediately after giving a pass each player runs round behind and to the other end of the line to receive and continue the practice. No. 1 starts by passing to No. 2 and immediately runs to the other end of the line. No. 2 then passes to No. 3 and follows quickly after No. 1,

then No. 3 followed by No. 4 so that as the line moves from one end of the pitch to the other the players keep up the pass-and-run-round procedure.

(*b*) As for (*a*) but the passer runs round one player at a time until he reaches the other end. No. 1 passes to No 2 and runs round 2 to receive; he then passes to 3, and so on, till he is at the other end.

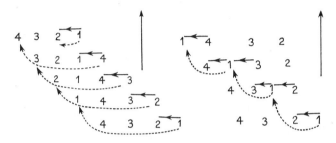

5. *Inside Pass Practice*—Players are arranged in lines of three, the middle man No. 2 holding the ball. As the

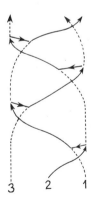

line begins to move along the field, No. 2 runs diagonally to the right to cross in front of No. 1, who veers to the left into the middle to receive the inside pass from No. 2.

31

No. 1 continues to the left to cross in front of No. 3, who now veers to the right to become the middle man and receives the inside pass from No. 1. No. 3 then runs across No. 2, then No. 2 across No. 1, and so on.

6. *Reverse Pass Practice*—As in No. 5 but using the reverse pass instead of the orthodox pass inside.

7. *Swing or Turning Pass Practice*—As in Nos. 5 and 6 but using the turn pass as the players cross.

8. *Running and Passing in Fours*—Outside players take reverse pass. This practice is similar to Nos. 5, 6, and 7 above except that four players are involved simulating two centres and two wings, and that one orthodox pass is made between each 'scissors' movement. Players continually change places from centre to wing and wing to centre to ensure that each player has a turn at being passer and receiver.

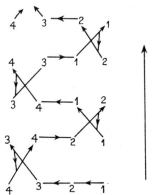

9. *Casual Passing Practice*—Players move around in no set order giving and taking passes *ad lib.* and varying the type of passes as much as possible. The greater the number and variety of passes the better.

10. *Unopposed Rugby*—Three opponents only to oppose the scrums.

Passing from the Ground

1. *Orthodox Pass*—Players in pairs. (*a*) The passer with the ball on the ground stands with his feet in the correct position for the pass. When ready he picks up and passes to his partner, who stands some distance away to his right or left. Partner then repeats the procedure and passes back to No. 1.

(*b*) As in (*a*) but receiver starts to run when he sees the passer bend to make the pass.

(*c*) As in (*a*) and (*b*) but the passer stands a few feet away from the ball so that the ball is situated between the two players, and on a signal given by either player he quickly steps to the ball using the correct footwork and passes to the receiver who starts running on the same signal.

2. As in 1 (*a*), (*b*), and (*c*) using swing, dive and reverse passing.

3. *Target Passing*—Post, or mark on wall waist-high.

Passing Practice Against Opponents

1. *Intercepting in Threes*—Players arranged in groups of three. Nos. 1 and 2 pass the ball from one to the other moving in any direction while No. 3 tries to

intercept. If No. 3 gains possession the last passer takes his place as interceptor. Variations (i) keeping the ball below head height, (ii) to touch the ball gives interceptor possession, (iii) to touch the man, or ball while in possession gives interceptor possession.

2. *Team Passing*—2 *v*. 2, 3 *v*. 3 etc. Players arranged in groups of four. 1 and 2 pass the ball among themselves while 3 and 4 try to intercept it. This is best done in a limited space to discourage running too far and encourage quick passing. Counting the number of consecutive passes will add to the interest of the game, each pair tries to gain more passes than the other. Teams could be increased to three-, four-, and five-a-side.

3. *Circle Pass Out*—One centre player, four passers, and four interceptors. Two circles are drawn one within the other with radii of 6 feet and 9 feet respectively and the players are arranged as in the diagram.

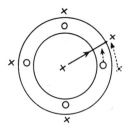

The ball is passed back and forth between the centre player and the passers while the interceptors try to gain possession. Passers and interceptors change places after a short period.

4. *Two Attackers v. One Defender*—Orthodox Pass—no tackling at first. The attackers, one of which holds the ball, stand 25 yards away from the defender. The attack and defence move forward and the object is for the player holding the ball to draw the defender and then pass to his colleague for an unchallenged run to the line. This demands of the passer, judgement of speed and distance, and good timing and accuracy in passing. It is surprising how difficult it is for many players to execute this fairly simple practice correctly. They either delay the pass to such an extent as to be tackled in possession or pass so early as to give the defender time to cross and challenge the receiver. Many, too, are so concerned with the approach of the defender and the thought of being tackled that they fail to look at the receiver when passing, with the result that the pass goes astray. It is therefore very important that young players get the opportunity to practise these skills, at first against 'token' opposition, and then to simulate more and more the true conditions of the game.

Wrong, pass made too early

5. *Three Attackers v. Two Defenders*. Procedure as for 4.

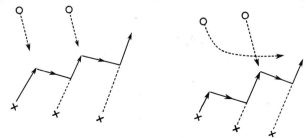

Wrong, first pass made too
early

6. *Four Attackers v. Three Defenders*

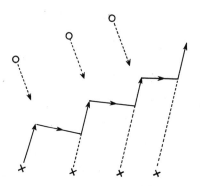

7. *Two Attackers v. One Defender*—Reverse Pass

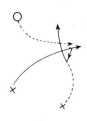

8. *Three Attackers v. Two Defenders*

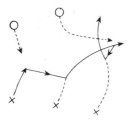

9. *Two Attackers v. Two Defenders*

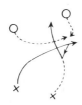

10. *Touch and Pass Seven-a-side.* Played across half the pitch. No scrums or line-outs. Drop kick to start and restart the game after a score. A short kick back to a colleague is used after an infringement, e.g. not passing the ball immediately after being touched by an opponent, forward pass, offside etc., otherwise no kicking. The ball may be thrown to any member of the team from touch.

11. *Modified Rugby Seven-a-side.* Played across half pitch. No tight scrums or line-outs. Drop kick to start and restart the game after a score. No kicking forward allowed but it may be heeled back after a tackle if a pick-up is not possible. A short kick back to a colleague is used after an infringement, e.g. forward pass, offside etc.

The ball may be thrown to any member of the team from touch.

12. *Rugby Seven-a-side*. Rugby Rules.

Passing Relay Races

1. *Line Passing Relay*. Players arranged in teams of four, No. 1 holding the ball. The ball is passed along the line to No. 4 who runs up behind the team to take No. 1's place as the team moves up one place. The passing continues until each player has run and until No. 1 returns to the head of the team.

2. *Wheel Relay*. Teams of four are arranged facing clockwise as in the diagram. No. 1 with the ball races round the wheel and returns to No. 4's place. The ball is then passed along the line to No. 2 who also runs round, and so on until all have completed their turn and returned to their original team places with No. 1 holding the ball. Players move up one place to make room on the inside for the runner.

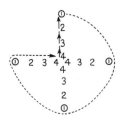

3. *Catch and Pass Relay*. Teams of five or six. No. 1 stands, holding the ball, between lines A and B as in

the diagram while the rest of the team stand behind Line A and facing Line B. No. 2 runs to take a pass from No. 1 and continues to Line B to touch it with the ball. On his way back to touch off No. 3 he returns a pass to No. 1. No. 3 then runs and the game continues until all the players have had a turn.

After his turn No. 2 takes No. 1's place and No. 1 joins the end of the team as runner.

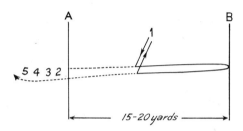

4. *Scrum-half Pass Relay.* Teams as in 3, except that No. 2 stands on line B holding the ball. No. 2 kicks or rolls the ball along the ground to No. 1 who picks up and passes to No. 3. The latter should time the start of his run according to the movements of the ball and

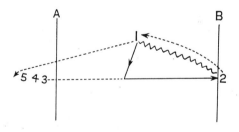

the passer. After the pass No. 1 joins the end of the team. No. 2 takes his place as passer and No. 3 runs to the line and kicks or rolls the ball to No. 2, who should then be in position to act as scrum-half. The race continues in this way until all have had a turn as catcher, roller, and passer.

The three other types of passes should be introduced in the race when a good standard of ability in them has been achieved in the simpler practices.

Passing from a Tackle

In order to keep up and press home the attack the player in possession should always try to pass, ideally, before he is tackled, to someone who is in a better position than himself. This may not always be possible and he may often find himself unintentionally or some-times even deliberately running into a tackle before the receiver is in position to take the pass. This does not mean that the attack should end here. Providing that the passer has both hands on the ball and does not allow the tackler to smother it by pinning his arm to the body, the pass can still be given even as the attacker falls in the tackle. Just as the tackle is made, both arms and the ball should be carried upward and well above the point of contact of the tackle and the tackler's clutches so that a pass may still be given. (N.B. A player must not pass from a completed tackle, i.e. when a player is brought down and held, or, when a player is held so that he cannot pass or play the ball.) In far too many players self-preservation inhibits all thought of passing under those circumstances and in-evitably scores of promising attacks peter out in the tackles. The following practices may help then to eliminate this fault by first concentrating on the pass and then turning the thought to falling correctly.

1. *Kneeling Pass.* In pairs. The passer kneels facing half right (or left) and passes as the body falls forward on to the hands, or the impact of the fall may be taken on the whole length of the forearms and open hands.

2. *Standing Pass*—as in 1 but facing front.

3. *Walking Pass.*

4. *Running Pass.* In this pass momentum of the run will carry the body forward during the fall, and it may be better to tuck and roll in a relaxed way to minimize the force of impact against the ground.

5. *Stationary Pass in a Tackle.* In threes. The third player assumes the tackling position on the passer and drives him over with his shoulder while keeping a firm grip round his legs. As the passer falls he passes.

6. *Walking Pass in a Tackle.* The passer goes through the procedure raising the ball clear of the tackler before the pass.

7. *Running Pass in a Tackle.* As in 6, running. A slow run first.

Catching a High Ball

1. Individual throwing upward and catching. Emphasis should be on keeping the eyes on the ball, and the correct position of the feet, arms, and hands, and on the 'body give' to cushion the impact of the ball against the body.

2. In pairs. No. 1 lobs for No. 2 to catch. No. 2 lobs for No. 1 etc.

3. In pairs. No. 1 lobs a short ball for No. 2 to run forward to catch before it bounces.

4. In pairs. No. 1 lobs to No. 2's right or left or over his head. No. 2 turns to move under the ball.

See also kicking activities, as kicking should now be included in the catching practices.

5. In pairs. No. 1 lobs to No. 2 and follows up to harass No. 2. At first No. 1 should delay his follow-up to give No. 2 sufficient time to make sure of a safe catch, but as skill and confidence increase he should be given less and less time so that the practice demands from him more and more concentration on the ball.

6. In threes. No. 1 lobs to No. 2, who passes to No. 3 before being tackled in possession by No. 1, who follows up.

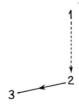

This simulates a situation where the full-back is under pressure and cannot kick to touch or evade in time, but finds that he can pass to a player (centre- or fly-half) who has dropped back to help or to start a counter-attack.

Springbok combines a hand-off and swerve to evade a British Lion

British Lion wing puts a South African wing off balance with a side-step

3/Kicking

KICKING seems to be one of the most popular of rugby fundamentals, yet very few players possess skill in it above the average. To kick a rugger ball requires very little skill, perhaps that is why it is so popular, but good, effective kicking is an art. It requires thought and much practice.

The Punt

Rugby is a handling game. That should be the prominent thought when players contemplate punting. No points can be directly derived from it, yet the punt to touch and the punt ahead in attack are both grossly over-used in rugby today. The punt ahead, in particular, is typical of the fatuous use of kicking in rugby. In most cases it serves only as a means of throwing away possession and giving the opponents the opportunity to hit back in attack. The best teams possess players who are great handlers and runners and therefore they very seldom deem it necessary to kick. Other teams have players whose handling is below par and therefore they kick a great deal. Punting is very often a sign of weakness in handling and attacking skill.

Holding the Ball

The ball is held in both hands with its forward point aimed in the direction of the intended kick. For a right-footed kick to the left touch-line, the ball should be turned slightly to the left with its forward point a little lower than the rear point. Probably the most popular hold is to place the right hand on top of the rear half of the ball so that the fingers, comfortably spread and pointing forward, extend just over the lace. The left hand supports it halfway along underneath its left side.

For a left-footed kick to the right touch-line the left hand would be on top, with the right hand supporting under the right side.

The Kick

The player steps forward on the left foot and swings the right leg through with a strong, fast extension of the knee. The ankle is extended with the foot turned inward slightly so that both foot and ball are in alignment.

As the leg swings through, the left hand is withdrawn from under the ball and the right hand aids its downward movement and virtually places it on to the kicking foot. For a long low kick, the point of contact between ball and foot is nearer the ground, the ankle is even more strongly extended, and the follow-through is more in a forward direction than for a kick which is shorter and higher.

The Torpedo Kick

This is a punt with spin on the ball so that it revolves point-first through the air round its longitudinal axis. The object is to decrease wind resistance and therefore gain distance. The mechanics of the kick are the same as in the ordinary punt, but the points of contact differ. Both ball and foot are in alignment and turned inward slightly. The contact surface of the foot is from the highest point of the instep outward. If the kick is made with a soft-toed boot, only the three outside toes feel the contact with the ball. The contact surface on the ball is a little to the left of the underneath centre seam. The force applied to one side of the ball imparts a spin in the opposite direction. A right-footed kick strikes the ball underneath its left side and imparts a spin to the right. Although the swing through of the kicking leg is straight forward, the force of impact between ball and foot causes the leg to swing inward in the follow-through.

The Punt Ahead in Attack

The kick should be aimed so that the chances of retrieving the ball are very good indeed, otherwise the kick should not be attempted, and ideally it should be high enough to give the retrieving player time to run under the ball and take it as it descends.

The Grubber Kick

This is a short punt along the ground aimed to pass through a gap between the defenders. Regaining possession depends on the antics of the ball or on the ability of the retrieving player to pick up. Occasionally the ball bounces conveniently to a height where it can be taken without difficulty. When this does not occur it must be picked up at speed or dribbled.

The body and head must be well over the ball during

the kick in order to keep it low. Some players prefer to employ the drop-kick method for the grubber kick instead of the punt method.

The Drop Kick

This kick produces points, and therefore it should be practised to perfection and manœuvres evolved so that during a game the kicker can be given the most favourable opportunities for success. One success may decide the difference between winning and losing.

The ball is held laterally in a near-upright position, leaning slightly toward the kicker, more by the fingers than by the palms of the hands. Many good drop-kickers hold the ball with the fingers placed roughly halfway between the points and across the seams pointing in a forward and downward direction, while others prefer to place the fingers along the seams.

For a right-foot kick the kicker steps forward on the left foot and carries the ball forward and away from the body. The ball is then dropped to the ground to land point-first, still leaning toward the kicker, and is kicked just as it begins to rise. The point of landing is about a foot's length in front and slightly to the right of the non-kicking foot. The kicking foot is strongly extended in alignment with the ball, and the whole length of the instep makes contact with the ball. If the kicker is well balanced and the kick perfectly aimed and timed, the follow-through will be good. The follow-through in any kick is the aftermath of the primary action, and is of no consequence. The predominant consideration should be the aiming and timing of the kick, and if these are accurate the follow-through will also be accurate. Watching the ball is essential to both aiming and timing in kicking.

The Place Kick

If goals can occasionally be kicked from seemingly improbable places why not oftener? The kicker has only to reproduce over and over again the technique of the successful kick. In order to do this the kicker must first develop the 'feeling' for the movements when the correct technique is produced and know and re-member the reasons why it was brought about. At first the feeling will be weak and the knowledge little, but with practice both will become stronger and more easily recognized. That, of course, is not the whole answer. Extraneous influences may effect the results. The technique of a particular kick might be accurate but a sudden gust of wind might take the ball off course and the kick fail, or, where a kick with a dry ball might succeed, a kick from the same point using a ball which is wet and muddy may fail because the player lacks the extra power to give distance to the heavier ball.

Extra practice might not result in one hundred per cent success but it will certainly add to previous suc-cesses. Improvement in a skill through practice is a physiological fact.

Placing the Ball

There are two methods of placing the ball. One way is to stand it on one of its points with slight variation of lean either forward or backward. The other is to lay it almost flat with its forward point aimed in the direc-tion of the kick.

48

For the upright method a U-shaped hole is made in the ground with the mouth of the U facing the direction of the kick. The lower point of the ball is placed into it. Whether the ball leans forward or backward is a matter of individual choice. The non-kicking foot is placed a little to the side and behind the ball and in this type of kick the kicking toe contacts the ball below its centre as the leg begins its upward arc. This force applied to the lower half of the ball gives rapid elevation but reduces the amount of forward force. It is the method most commonly used for short kicks when accuracy and quick elevation and not distance is the aim, although some kickers use it for both short and long kicks.

For the longer kicks the second method is generally adopted. For this the mouth of the U faces the kicker and the ball is supported by the raised sides of the U and placed so that the foremost point cuts through the air during flight. Some very successful kickers prefer to 'tee' up the ball on a U-shaped mound of earth to give that extra elevation to ensure an accurate contact between the toe and the ball's lower point. The placing of the non-kicking foot is the same as in the first method, but in this all the force imparted by the kicking foot, if accurately applied, is in a forward upward direction and should give added distance.

Run-Up

The length of run-up is a matter of individual choice, and is often dependent on the length of the kick. For correct foot placing it is better to keep the approaching strides to a minimum, within reason, and to work out a stride plan so that the number of running steps remain constant, say three strides for the short and five for the longer kicks. It is recommended that the approach to the ball be on a straight line, although some successful kickers use a curved approach. In all methods of kicking, the speed with which the kicking leg swings through the arc is important. Providing that the timing of impact is correct, the faster the leg swings the greater the force imparted to the ball, and greater force correctly applied means greater distance.

Schoolboys should use a light ball when learning to kick.

Kicking Practices

Punting

1. Correct hold of the ball.

2. Tossing the ball into the air, catching, and assuming the correct hold quickly ready for the kick.

3. Correct position of the ball on the foot. The curve should fit into the instep with both foot and ball in alignment.

4. Two-step punt to partners. Players in pairs standing about 15 yards apart. For a right-footed kick the kicker steps forward on the right foot, then on the left, and as it comes to the ground he swings through and kicks with the right. The second step is quicker than the first and is more like a short running stride. Step right then left and kick with the right.

5. As in 4 with a left-footed kick. Step left, right, and kick with the left.

6. As in 4 and 5 with partner standing 25–30 yards away. Kicking for accuracy. The kicker should aim to

punt so that partner can field without having to move from his standing position.

7. Touch-kicking in pairs. Any of the lines marked on the field can be used as touch-lines. Emphasis, at first, should be on accuracy of touch-finding and not on distance. Two kicks should be made with the weaker foot to every one with the better foot.

8. Target touch-finding. The kicker decides on a target distance at which to aim, e.g. halfway line or a point between the halfway line and 25-yard line.

9. Touch-finding through the goal posts. Kicking along the try line from a wide angle at first to punt the ball first bounce between the uprights. Gradually narrow the angle to kick from nearer the try line, and experiment on methods of curving the ball between the uprights.

10. Running, short punt ahead and catch. Gradually increase the length of the punt.

11. As in 10 using 6 foot post as the defender to beat. Running, short punt, run round the post, and catch, or to pick up at speed.

12. As in 11. In pairs. A player as defender.

Specialised Practices

1. Torpedo kick.

2. Catch and kick, in pairs. No. 1 kicks to No. 2 and follows up quickly. No. 2 fields and kicks to touch before being tackled in possession by No. 1. (At first No. 1 should not run up to harass No. 2 too quickly.)

3. Catch—evade and kick. In pairs. No. 1 kicks to No. 2 and follows up quickly. No. 2 fields, evades No. 1, and kicks to touch. In the initial stages of this

practice the follow-up player should give No. 2 plenty of time in which to catch the ball and prepare himself to evade. Gradually less and less time should be given to the catcher as his confidence and ability improve.

4. As in 3 with two or three follow-up players.

Drop Kicking

1. Standing drop kick. The player stands with the kicking foot raised behind. The first objective is to develop the timing of the contact between foot and the rising ball, and perhaps the best way to achieve this is to use a soccer ball because the kicker can be assured of a true bounce every time. If the activity takes place on a hard surface and the kick is directed to a wall, the practice can be speeded up and the kicker is relieved of the task of retrieving. The player need not stand more than 3 or 4 yards away from the wall, with the emphasis on timing and not on strength of kick.

2. Correct hold and angle of drop. Rugby ball. The ball should be dropped so that it bounces with a slight lean toward the kicker.

3. Standing drop kick. In pairs. Players should stand about 10 yards apart. The kicker stands with the kicking foot raised behind and concentrates on a true bounce and timing.

4. Two-step drop kick. In pairs. Players stand 20–25 yards apart. Steps as in punting. Step right, then left, and kick with the right. Repeat with the left foot. Step left, then right, and kick with the left.

5. Drop-kick practice at goal. From easy positions at first with alternate feet, gradually increasing the angle and distance.

6. Drop kick along the try line. Object is to try and hit the near upright.

7. Snap drop kick at goal after a catch. No delay in holding the ball.

8. Pressure practice—four to six consecutive drop kicks at goal from successive passes quickly given by partner.

9. Catch—evade follow-up player and drop kick for goal.

Place Kicking

1. Correct placing of the ball in the U-shaped hole or 'tee'.

2. Correct placing of non-kicking foot and the contact of kicking foot with the ball.

3. Two-step place kick to partner. Steps as in punting. Step right, then left, and kick with the right.

4. Place kicking for goal. From easy positions at first, gradually narrowing the angle and increasing distance.

5. Place kicking along the try line. The ball is placed on the try line and the kick directed along it to try and hit the near upright. The approach should also be along the line, and by this stage the kicker should have decided upon a workable stride pace in the run-up.

4/*Evading*

THE methods of evading are side-step, swerve, hand-off, and change of pace (which includes coming to an abrupt stop to let the would-be tackler rush past in front). These are skills at which all players wish they were expert, yet only two reasons prevent them from being good at them all. The first is the inability to analyse the mechanics involved and, the lack of self-discipline to practise them hard enough. All these skills should be part of every player's repertoire.

The Side-step

Some believe that unless players are born side-steppers they will never be able to side-step. That is a complete fallacy. Not only can players be taught, or teach themselves, to side-step off either foot but they can also be taught to master an effective double side-step; that is, two side-steps in two consecutive steps, from right to left and back again to the right, or vice versa, to make a defender move the wrong way. A well-balanced defender has the body weight equally distributed on both feet, and is able to move either to the right or left with equal ease to deal with an attacker who is running straight toward him with very little room for manœuvre on either side. The attacker's only means of going through is to make the defender step to one side to make room for him to continue on a near straight-ahead path. This is an ideal situation in which to use the double side-step. The first will move the defender in the same direction as the side-step and the second, which follows in the next stride, will take the attacker back again on the original path and through.

Practices for the Side-step

1. *Standing on the Right Leg,* bend the knee slightly and push off to the left to land on the left leg, then an immediate push off the left leg back on to the right and continue. The action, as in the side-step proper, is more of a glide sideways than a hop. High hopping or jumping sideways should be discouraged from the outset. Keep the body low.

A harder leg drive in this practice will carry the body further to the side and help to develop strength and speed in the leg action.

2. As in 1—but moving slowly forward on a zig-zag path as the body is driven off one leg on to the other.

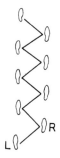

3. *The Three-Step Method—Walking.* The player stands facing a little to the right for a side-step off the right foot.

First Sequence

    1. A stride to the front with the right leg.

    2. A stride with the left.

    3. Another stride with the right and as the foot comes to the ground the leg bends slightly and drives the body forward and to the left on to the left foot. Therefore the side-step is made on every third count.

When the left foot comes to the ground pointing in the new direction it will represent the first stride in the second sequence.

    1. Left foot.

    2. Right foot.

    3. Left foot and drive to the right.

The practice is continued on a zig-zag path in sequence of three strides.

4. *As in* 3—Running slowly at first.

5. *Three-step Method—Running*. Posts should now be used to represent defenders. Since a player, after a side-step, hardly ever returns on to the original path, the posts should be placed alternately, as in the diagram and at the appropriate distance apart.

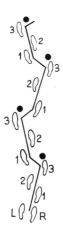

The ball should sometimes be carried during this practice, and transferred to the side away from the post when executing the side-step so that the near hand is free to hand off.

6. *Five-step Method—Walking and later Running*. In this practice five strides are taken between each side-step.

7. *Free Side-stepping Practice.* Side-stepping imaginary defenders varying the number of strides between side-steps. Usually the last two strides before the side-step are shortened to check speed ready for the drive, but, ideally the side-step should be made without shortening the strides and loss of speed.

8. *Side-step Against an Opponent.* Some coaches advocate bringing the rear foot up to the front foot immediately after the side-step. This seems to be an unnecessary practice to encourage, for it means a loss in distance of one stride length. The foot which is brought up could be more profitably employed in going straight through into the next stride.

The Double Side-step

1. *Three-step Method—Walking.*

(*a*) As in the foregoing practices but two consecutive side-steps on the third and fourth counts.

(*b*) Starting with the left foot so that the first side-step is to the right off the left foot.

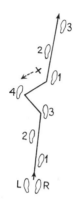

2. *Three-step Method—Running.*

3. *Double Side-step Against Opponent.* In pairs. This is not a high-speed evasive tactic because of the difficulty in maintaining balance, and if the first side-step is performed too quickly, it will not give the defender sufficient time to see and follow it.

The Swerve

There is no break in the running stride in the swerve like that in the side-step, only a change in the direction of the run. The body weight is moved sideways and away from the defender, aided by the driving action of the legs and feet, on the outside of the far foot and the inside of the near foot. The body lean is always to the inside of the line of swerve and the feet drive in the outward direction. In a swerve to the right the body lean is to the right while the feet drive to the left, and

59

vice versa. Running round in a small circle will give players the feeling of inward body lean.

The mechanics of the swerve need not be analysed and practised at walking pace as in the side-step. Even children of 9 or 10 years of age will swerve quite well if asked to run in and out of a row of obstacles. But to be able to swerve really well and use it as an effective tactic needs much practice in order to develop the essential timing, sharp change of direction, and smooth body sway from side to side without diminishing running speed. In fact, players should endeavour to accelerate through the swerve.

Timing the swerve is important. If it starts too early the defender will be given time to react, forcing the attacker to make a much wider sweep to avoid the tackle. The wider the sweep, the less chance the swerve has of succeeding, especially against a defender of equal speed. It should be delayed until just before the defender is in the position to commit himself to the tackle, or he must be made to check his speed and straighten his approach by a straightening of the attacker's run toward the defender before the swerve. Therefore, the direction of approach before the swerve is as important as timing. A diagonal approach, for a swerve in the same general direction, results in a wide sweeping curve, and the defender will find no difficulty in accelerating round it after his man. But to make the defender run straight at his man offers the best possible situation for an effective swerve and, once beaten, the defender is placed in the worst possible position to try to redeem his mistake, that of changing direction completely. The more acute the angle of the defender's approach the easier he will be to beat. The curve of the attacker's run will be much sharper and the defender will find it necessary to stop, turn about, and pick up speed again. In nearly every case there will be little the defender can do for he will have been decisively beaten.

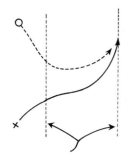

| Width of curve in diagonal approach | Width of curve in straight approach |

Practices

1. Running in and out a row of posts placed about 8–10 yards apart. As skill improves the posts can be brought closer together to encourage a sharper turn. Emphasis should be on maintaining speed and a smooth running stride.

2. As in 1 carrying a ball. The ball should be transferred from side to side away from the posts.

3. As in 2. Going through the motions of handing-off each post.

4. Running in and out posts placed in casual order to develop greater manœuvrability at speed.

The Hand-off

The hand-off is a sharp, vigorous stretching of the arm to ward off a tackle, and should be directed to the nearest solid point, i.e. top of the head, face, or chest, on the oncoming defender. Timing and accuracy are of vital importance. The elbow should be bent and brought close to the side with the hand open and roughly at shoulder height. The stretching should be quick and decisive when the tackler is at arm's length distance. If the tackle is high the target is either the face or chest, but in a low one the hand-off is directed downwards and outward to the top of the head.

If the tackle is determined, well timed and directed, then it is essential that the hand-off be used in conjunction with a swerve to cushion the force of impact. Unless this is done the chances are that the hand-off will fail, because the combined momentum of the tackler's run in and dive, plus his body weight, will

n Gwillian, the Welsh forward, jumps high to execute a one-handed
op catch. The left hand at shoulder height is ready to support the ball
as it is brought down by the right hand

Clifford, the Swansea forward gets the ball down from a line-out

either force the attacker's arm to bend, so that the tackler gets within grasping distance, or bowl him over. The attacker could use this momentum to his own advantage by momentarily allowing it to drive him sideways and forward, while still keeping the tackler at arm's length in his dive.

Practices

1. *Stationary Practice*. Players standing in pairs. Practise hand-off to the padded chest and the top of the head. For the latter, one player stands with the body bent forward. The hand-off should not be vigorous for this. Spare sweater for pad.

2. As in 1, but attacker walks past standing defender.

3. As in 2—running slowly.

4. Both players use walking and slow-running approach.

5. Incorporate handing-off in tackling practice.

Change of Pace

There are three ways in which change of pace may be used to beat an opponent, and their success depends upon the ability of the attacker to develop great pace very quickly. They are:

1. A straightforward acceleration to top speed.

2. Change to a slower pace followed by acceleration to top speed.

3. Very quickly stopping, followed by acceleration to top speed.

(*a*) In the first method the attacker should accelerate when the defender approaches tackling distance. The sudden increase of speed may catch the defender off his guard when he is in a state of preparedness for the tackle, and this might cause him to throw himself into an abortive dive in a desperate attempt to stop his man. At least the attacker should gain a few yards, since there will be a very short space of time before the defender interprets the change of pace and reacts accordingly by increasing his own speed. A slight swerve could be used in conjunction with the acceleration.

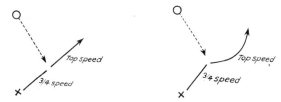

(b) The attacker decreases speed to check the defender who is likely to straighten his run a little to cover a possible inside break, and then accelerates to top speed when he sees the defender's speed decreasing. The defender is again at a disadvantage since he cannot increase his own speed until after he has interpreted the attacker's tactics, and by that time the attacker should have gained those vital few yards and be through the opening made outside his man. The attacker could also use the inside and outside swerves in conjunction with the decrease and increase of speed, respectively.

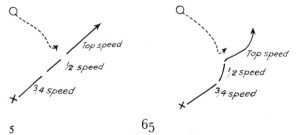

(*c*) This requires the attacker to come to a momentary dead stop so quickly, and at such a time that the defender can do nothing to prevent himself over-running his man, it may be more than a yard or two from the point of intended tackle. The attacker then accelerates through the gap he has created by displacing a defender. He may choose to change direction slightly.

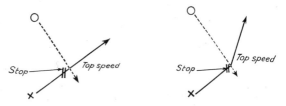

A strong determined runner can often crash through a tackle by running into deliberate collision with the tackler. Shortly before impact the runner lowers himself into a bunched position so that the hips (sometimes protected by the near arm bent and held close to the side) are slightly below the plane of the tackler's dive, and, at the right time, he drives the hips and body sideways and upwards into the tackler in an attempt to knock him off before he has time to wrap the arms around his body. One of these has often proved successful in revealing a weak spot in the opponent's defence.

Deception

Body movements or feints may cause him to hesitate and slow down, or change direction slightly. The dummy pass is an obvious one. Others include: dummy swerves, by swaying the hips and running with the feet crossing the line of run; dummy side-step, by lowering the body slightly over the forward foot as it comes to the ground and by shortening the running strides; dummy kick ahead, by first lifting and then lowering the ball accompanied by a very quick adjustment of the feet as if preparing to punt. All these should be followed by an acceleration if full advantage is to be taken of the defender's hesitancy or indecision.

Continuous Evading Practices

1. *The Triangle.* Three posts are placed in the ground to form a triangle whose sides are 25–30 yards long.

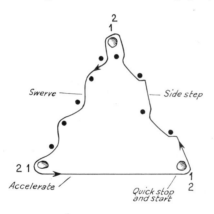

Along the first side other posts are placed alternatively as for side-step practice No. 5; on the second side more posts are placed as for swerve practice; the third side is left free. At least six players are necessary to keep the practice moving continuously, two at each corner, with No. 1 holding a ball. The object is to run round the triangle practising the evading skills, i.e. side-step, swerve, and acceleration and quick stop, on the way. The three No. 1's will start together (each running along a different side of the triangle) and when they return they pass the ball to No. 2 in their own corner. No. 2's start as soon as they receive the ball. The three No. 2's follow suit while No. 1's remain in the corner until No. 2 returns, and repeat. To make it competitive players should try to catch and pass the man in front, or try to be the first team to finish after all players have completed three or four circuits.

5/Tackling

TACKLING requires confidence, courage, force, timing and, in the tackler's own interest, correct technique. Some young players abound in courage and throw themselves at the opponent yet fail to bring off an effective tackle because of incorrect timing and technique and may even hurt themselves in the process. Some enjoy tackling as much as any other form of play in rugby and get as much pleasure out of it as making a brilliant break-through. And at the other extreme there are those who don't like tackling and avoid it if they can.

The technique remains the same whether the tackle is made from the front, side, or rear, but the point of aim will differ slightly. Just before the tackle the eyes should be on the point of impact. The tackler's run-in and drive provides the momentum and force; the shoulder, being the 'hammer-head' of the tackle, transmits the force to the attacker, and, as the shoulder makes contact the arms close tightly round the legs and pull.

Side Tackle

In the tackle from the side, the point of aim should be the thighs just above the knees where the thick muscles afford some protection for the shoulder. The head should be placed behind the opponent's thighs and the tackler should aim to drive the shoulder through the legs to ensure maximum impact.

Rear Tackle

When tackling from behind, the point of aim should be the buttocks with the head placed on the side of the disengaged shoulder. The arms close round the legs and may be allowed to slide down to knee level. This higher point of contact is recommended to avoid being struck by the feet as they come upwards in the back-heeling action in running.

The Front Tackle

In the front, head-on, or crash tackle, the lower part of the stomach should be the point at which to aim. To get the best effect from this tackle it must be decisive. The tackler's momentum should be such that it knocks the attacker over backwards. This means that the speed of the tackler's run-in, and the force of his drive must be greater and overcomes the forward momentum of his opponent. Two or three hard, well-timed tackles of this kind, in the early stages of the game, may cause certain players to give out hurried and inaccurate passes in subsequent movements.

Stationary Tackle

When the tackler is stationary or nearly so he does one of two things. For the first he stands slightly crouched on a stable support, i.e. feet slightly astride with one foot braced back. Just before contact is made he straightens both legs, drives his shoulder in, stops his man, and bowls him over backwards with the tackler on top. For the second, he allows the attacker to come abreast, makes his tackle and lets the runner's momentum carry him backwards while still retaining the grip on the legs. As the tackler falls backwards he should endeavour to turn toward the engaged shoulder so that he finishes on top of his opponent. The first method must often be used when defending very near the goal line as an alternative to the smother tackle.

The Smother Tackle

The smother tackle is used when the tackler's aim is to take man and ball. Its purpose is to prevent the opponent passing the ball, and therefore it simply means that the tackler aims high to pin the opponent's arms to his side.

Manœuvring for a Tackle

The approach to a tackle varies according to circumstances. When approaching a man in possession who is well prepared to take evasive action, the run should be one of caution, balance, and preparedness to change direction and speed suddenly. A player rushing in from some distance away may give the attacker ample time to effect a counter. Only in the last few yards when the tackler has manœuvred his man into a position of no escape should he accelerate and crash in. When the attacker's attention is on receiving or giving a pass, the approaching run and final acceleration can be started earlier and this enables the tackler to apply greater force to the tackle.

Tackling Practices

The first objective in teaching young players to tackle is to accustom them to a certain amount of rough and tumble. Some boys take quite naturally to tackling and need only polish up the technique while others must be introduced to it gradually and need much encouragement.

Body contact activities like pair contests for strength, and wrestling are ready-made practices, and certain simple ball games modified to suit the purpose can also be useful.

1. Contests.

2. Wrestling on the ground. The winner pins his man on the ground for a count of ten.

3. Modified Chinese Wall—The wall is represented by the area between two parallel lines about 10 yards apart. One or more players stand on the wall to defend it while the rest of the players (invaders) stand outside the lines. On a signal the invaders try to cross the wall as many times as they can without being caught by the defenders. When an invader is caught he becomes a defender and helps to catch the remaining players. A defender is not allowed outside the lines. A player is caught when he is held and lifted off the ground by one or more defenders, but the invaders can struggle to break free while they still have some part of the body in contact with the ground. The player who crosses the wall the greatest number of times wins.

4. Stationary tackling. In pairs, one player assumes the tackling position on his partner, i.e. Shoulder against the thighs, head behind and arms clasped tightly round the legs. The tackler pushes with his

shoulder by straightening the legs and at the same time pulls with the arms to drive his partner to the ground.

The side and rear tackle can be practised in this way.

5. Walking Tackle. As in 4, with tackler walking up to tackle stationary player.

6. As in 5. Both walking.

7. Walking tackle on dummy. Tackling dummies are not used as much as they should be. They need not be elaborate and can be made of sacks or old kit-bags filled with wood shavings or straw, and suspended from gallows or trees. It is better if they are fitted with a counter-weight and pulley or a spring arrangement for extension, or if not the bag could be the type that stands without support. Another arrangement is to suspend the dummy on a horizontal rope and construct the hanging device so that the dummy can be pulled along the rope to simulate a running player. This will be a better aid in timing the tackles.

8. As in 7 with a slow run approach, gradually increasing speed as confidence develops. The tackling practice should be with alternate shoulders to avoid the habit of tackling on one side only.

Further tackling practices should be done in conjunction with other rugby skills. Hard running tackling in cold blood is not a very satisfactory practice, particularly for the average boy who is being tackled. The tackle always seems much harder when the mind is fully conscious of it. It is far better if tackling can be introduced in some game form, e.g. modified tag and simple passing games and evading practices.

6/Picking Up

Picking Up

The ability to pick up has become increasingly important since the change in the Rugby Union Law concerning the method of bringing the ball into play after a tackle. But unfortunately many clubs have so far failed to take advantage of this new law, and the only reason is the lack of ability to pick up the loose ball. Many forwards are so unaccustomed to handling and picking up that they lack the confidence to attempt it during a game, and prefer to use the old method of playing the ball with the foot and leave the picking up to someone else.

This is a skill rarely performed well at speed for obvious reasons, therefore no training session should be considered complete without some practice in it.

The Pick-up Stance

To pick up on the right, the player places the right foot so that the ball is slightly to the right and just in front of the foot. The left foot is placed roughly in line with the right and about two foot lengths in front (the distance between the feet will obviously be greater in the running approach). The right and near hand is placed behind the ball ready to scoop it in a forward and upward direction into the left hand, which should

74

be just in front ready to receive the ball. It is doubtful if the most skilful players ever place both hands on the ball simultaneously when picking up at speed. The near hand does the major part of the work and the other helps to bring it under full control. In picking up on the left side the reverse procedure is adopted; left foot near the ball with the right foot in front, left hand behind the ball with the right in front. The footwork is the same when picking up with one hand. As far as getting down to the ball and maintaining balance are concerned it is easier to pick up with one hand, but of course much more skill is required in the actual pick-up. When both hands are used the remote hand brings with it the weight of the arm and shoulder of that side down and across the line of run and results in a more twisted crouched position of the body than when only one hand is used. In the one-handed pick-up, the remote hand and arm help to counter-balance the body lean to the pick-up side.

When a player is picking up on the run, the ball is actually picked up a fraction before the forward foot comes to the ground. When dealing with a rolling ball, players should try to avoid picking up across the direction of the roll but rather to pick up against or with the roll.

Grounding

The opposite to picking up is grounding and of course there is a correct way of grounding the ball on the run. The ball is placed on the ground just in front of and outside the foot on the side on which the grounding is to be made. Both hands will at first control the ball

75

in the lowering action and if the ball is to be grounded on the right side the right hand will be on top of the ball with the left supporting it underneath. When the ball has been lowered to about knee level the left hand is withdrawn and the right applies downward pressure to the ball and places it just in front and outside the right foot. Placing the ball very nearly coincides in timing with the placing of the right foot in the running stride.

Practices

1. Practise foot position.

2. *Walking Pick-up*. Players in three's with one ball walking clockwise round in a small circle. No. 1 picks up on the right side, and after walking a few steps grounds the ball for No. 2. No. 2 then picks up and grounds for No. 3, and so on. They should walk in an anti-clockwise direction for a pick-up on the left side. Emphasis on correct foot placing.

3. *Running Pick-up*. As in 2 but running slowly. Practise to right and left with both hands and then using only one hand.

4. *Picking up a Rolling Ball*. In pairs, facing the same way. No. 1 rolls the ball across and in front for No. 2 to run on to and pick up. No. 2 then rolls it forward and across for No. 1, and so on as they progress along the field.

5. *Pick-up and Pass*. In pairs—running. No. 1 rolls the ball forward and runs to pick it up and passes to No. 2. No. 2 then rolls, picks up, and passes back to No. 1, and so on. Speed of the running should be increased with improved skill.

6. *Picking up the Dribbled Ball with Side Approach.* In pairs. No. 1 dribbles the ball and allows it to advance 4 or 5 yards between kicks. No. 2 approaches from the dribbler's left, runs across his path to pick up with the right side nearer the ball.

7. As 6, approaching from the other side to pick up with the left side nearer the ball.

8. As in 6 and 7 with the ball kept nearer the dribbler's feet.

9. *Pick-up with Front Approach and Evade.* No. 1 dribbles and allows the ball to advance 4 or 5 yards or more depending on No. 2's skill. No. 2 approaches slowly from the front to pick up and evades the oncoming dribbler as if to start a counter attack.

10. As in 6–9 increasing the number of dribblers to simulate a forward foot rush.

Relays

1. *Pick-up Relay.* Teams of four standing behind line A facing line B. The ball is placed in front of the team midway between the lines. No. 1 runs to pick up and continues to line B to touch it with the ball, and then runs back to touch off No. 2, grounding the ball on the halfway mark on the way back. No. 2 then runs and No. 1 joins at the back of the team, and so on.

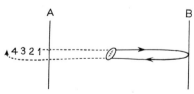

2. *Pick-up Rolling Ball Relay*. Arrangement of team as in 1. No. 1 runs and picks up on his way to line B. At the beginning of his return journey he rolls the ball along the ground for No. 2, who should start his run when the ball leaves No. 1's hands. No. 1 returns to stand behind the team. No. 2 rolls the ball on his way back for No. 3, and so on. The last player grounds the ball halfway between the lines to end the race.

3. *Pick-up and Pass Relay*. Teams of five. No. 1 stands between the lines to the right or left of the line of four holding the ball. The rest of the team stand behind line A facing line B. No. 1 rolls the ball along the ground toward No. 2, who runs forward to pick up, and when in the appropriate position passes the ball back to No. 1 and continues to line B to stand facing the team. No. 1, on receiving the pass, rolls for No. 3 who follows the same procedure as No. 2. The game ends when No. 5 crosses line B. The race can then be run in the opposite direction. The No. 1 should be changed after each race.

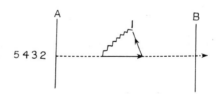

Picking up should be practised on both sides with both hands and then with one hand.

7 / *Dribbling and Falling*

GOOD dribbling is a matter of practice. Control of the ball depends on quickness and lightness on the feet and on nicely judged pushes and taps to keep it fairly close should a quick change of direction be necessary, and to make it a more hazardous task for the defence to fall and stop the dribble.

The dribbler should be moving on his toes the whole time with the head and body over the ball when it is kicked. Most of the dribbling is done with the inside of the feet and insteps, sometimes with the aid of the outside and shins. The taps and pushes should be in a forward and downward direction to ensure that the ball rolls along instead of bouncing. Allowing the ball to move too far ahead gives the defence the opportunity to pick up, and a pack of forwards closely bunched, who lose the ball give opponents a good opportunity to counter-attack.

Often after a short dribble it would be more advantageous for the attack if the ball were picked up and the attack continued by inter-passing. This necessitates precision in picking up and passing at speed, and therefore it should be incorporated into many of the dribbling practices.

1. Individual dribbling.
2. Dribbling in and out of obstacles.

3. Dribbling in pairs. No. 1 dribbles a short distance and passes to No. 2 who runs on a parallel path about 4 or 5 yards away.

4. Dribbling in groups of three to eight. Supporting players should back up on both sides and behind the dribbler.

5. Individual dribbling and picking up. Players dribble a short distance then pick up. The ball is then dropped in front and the procedure repeated, gradually speeding up the practice.

6. Dribbling, pick up, and pass. In pairs No. 1 dribbles a short distance then picks up and passes to No. 2 who runs on a parallel path 4 or 5 yards away. No. 2 then drops the ball, dribbles, picks up, and passes to No. 1, and so on, gradually speeding up the practice.

Falling

Falling, like tackling, requires confidence, courage, and timing.

The skill of falling on the ball is not difficult to learn. The important quality to achieve is the unhesitating and automatic decision to fall, no matter how near the dribbler's legs the ball might be. Some activities may appear frightening to many beginners, and to take part in them demands considerable will power. If through prudent coaching, boys achieve a measure of success fairly early, they will continue to practise the skill, and if the practice is sufficiently thorough the skill becomes automatic and the initial fear disappears. This is true in teaching boys to fall on the ball.

When stopping a foot rush the player's ideal approach is from the side so that he dives and falls across the path of the dribblers. He should land with his back to opponents, gather the ball into his body, and tuck in the head and knees so that only the curved back is presented to them. Should he get the opportunity to get up and run with the ball he will be able to do so quicker from this tucked position.

If the approach is from the front, the faller must dive over the ball with a twisting action to assume the correct position on the ground. The nearer he falls to the dribblers' legs the better. The dribbler may trip over the faller's body and this may give the latter the opportunity to get up with the ball and start an attack.

If the falling player is not held he may get up and run with the ball or play it with his feet while still on the ground, but unless he is able to do either of these he must release the ball and roll clear as soon as possible.

Practices

1. Assume correct position on the ground.

2. Falling on a stationary ball from kneeling or squat. Side and front approach.

3. As in 2 on a rolling ball. Players in pairs. No. 1 rolls or kicks the ball for No. 2 and vice versa.

4. As in 3. Falling from standing.

5. In pairs. No. 1 dribbles the ball at walking speed for No. 2 to fall. Players could use gym shoes in the early stages.

6. As in 5, gradually speeding up the dribbling.

7. Free dribbling and falling. Players divided into two groups 'fallers' and 'dribblers'.

8. Falling and getting up quickly with the ball to start an attack. Dribbler should deliberately trip over the faller.

L. Williams, the Cardiff scrum half kicks for touch

A Pontypool player kicks as he nears the touch-line

8 / Line-out

IT HAS been estimated that there are as many line-outs in a rugby game as there are tight and loose scrums put together. If this is true, it emphasizes the vast number of kicks to touch, most of them quite unnecessary because players take the line of least resistance when they lack enterprise and attacking skill. On an average not more than two or three forwards in any team have any line-out skill of consequence, and therefore it seems that the majority of forwards merely make up the formation of the line, defend if necessary, and take part in the ensuing loose scrum should the ball be brought down.

These two or three line-out experts are called 'specialists'. Usually they are the tallest men in the pack and have developed the necessary skill through practice. Even if they did not practise the art in the training sessions, they will have done so in games, because the ball is probably thrown to them far oftener than to the other forwards since they have the advantage in height. Height is the only natural attribute these specialists have over the other forwards. The skill is acquired. Therefore there is no reason whatsoever why every forward should not be a specialist, with the same ability to jump and pass back as the best of the tall men. Usually men are marked by opponents of approximately the same height and if a player has superior jumping ability and general line-out skill he has the advantage, and there is no reason why the ball should not be thrown to him occasionally. This means that the ball could be thrown to any one of eight forwards, tactics could be greatly varied and the tall men given an occasional respite. It must be remembered that they too have to push in the scrum, tackle, and run about as much as any of the other forwards, and to expect them to take all the responsibility of line-out work as well is asking a lot of them.

Stance

Stance in the line-out varies according to individual choice. Some players like to stand in a semi-crouched position with the arms bent and the hands at about shoulder level, some prefer standing fairly upright on the toes with the arms held above the shoulders, while others stand with the knees slightly bent and arms to the side.

The important thing is to stand in a position which best suits the individual player and which gives him the most powerful drive into the air.

Timing

Timing the jump is important. A player merely wastes energy if he jumps too early or too late or if the chances of reaching the ball are remote. If the ball looks like falling short or passing out of reach overhead he will do well to stay on the ground and prepare himself for the ensuing play.

Spring

The player who can jump highest has a distinct advantage. Spring can be developed through practice. It requires strength and mobility in the legs and an abundance of exercises are available to achieve these physical qualities. As a guide to jumping ability, players should try the following test. The jumper, with both feet flat on the ground with his arms fully stretched upward, stands under an object which can be adjusted vertically. The object is lowered until it touches the jumper's finger-tips and then raised 24–26 inches. The test is to jump to touch the underside of the object with the finger-tips of both hands, without preliminary and winding-up bounces. The object is adjusted for each individual according to his height.

Techniques

There are several methods employed to gain possession of the ball in the line-out and bring it into play. Most are fervently advocated for safe general use while the others are viewed doubtfully by a large number of coaches, old players etc. If the aim is to send the ball to the scrum-half, then it should always be done with the utmost expediency.

Forwards should always remember that the moment they gain possession of the ball in the line-out the defending threequarters begin to move forward in defence, and the longer the ball is retained by the forwards the more difficult it is going to be for their own halves and threequarters to attack and gain ground should the ball be subsequently passed to them from the line-out.

Method 1

The player jumps to catch the ball with both hands, turns toward his scrum-half and passes immediately after the catch, while still at the peak of his jump. The turn begins on the way up and ideally the player should be facing his scrum-half when giving his pass. Eyes should be on the ball until it is safely in the hands, then eyes on the catcher. This method is the quickest safe way because the ball is caught and passed with both hands. It requires much skill and practice and every forward should master it. It is the ideal method.

Method 2

The player jumps to catch the ball with both hands, descends, and passes to the scrum-half from chest or waist level. Unless he is quick to pass he is liable to be smother-tackled from behind and lose the advantage.

Method 3

After jumping to catch with both hands, the player descends with his back to the opponents, places his feet astride, and bends forward and downward with arms extended and the ball held near the ground. He either passes from ground level or drops the ball and kicks it with the inside of the foot to the scrum-half. With the body bent forward and arms extended in this way, the chances of the ball being smothered from behind are slight.

Method 4

After catching the ball and descending, the player drops it, a loose scrum is formed, and the ball is heeled back. Occasionally the catcher chooses to fall, taking the ball with him, with his back to the opponents and a loose scrum is formed over him.

Method 5

The player jumps to reach for the ball with one hand and without delaying it flicks or deflects it directly to the scrum-half. This method requires great accuracy and timing and should not be attempted unless the player has practised it to perfection. This is the quickest possible way of sending the ball from the line-out to the scrum-half, and there is no reason to condemn it, providing it succeeds say eight times out of ten. Occasionally the deflection is made to another forward who has moved slightly out of the line.

Method 6

The player jumps and employs the one-handed scoop catch. On landing he either passes or releases the ball for a loose scrum. This method of gaining possession is sometimes necessary when the vertical jump and catch with both hands is impracticable. For example, should the ball's flight be more to the opponent's side of the line-out, jumping to catch it with both hands might not be possible because other players are in the way or because of the subsequent loss of balance in the descent after a jump which was more sideways-upwards than directly upward. To deal with such a ball the player should jump vertically to ensure a balanced descent, reach for the ball with one hand, and scoop it downward to shoulder or chest level where the other hand is ready to give it full-support. This method obviously requires a great deal of skill, and should not be used until the player is satisfied that a very high level of proficiency has been attained in its execution.

There will be several occasions when the forwards will choose to retain the ball and employ their own tactics from the line-out. For example:

1. *Bunch and Take*

This is often employed to gain a few yards when the ball has been gained by the defending team in a line-out near the try line. After catching the ball the player descends facing his opponents, and his colleagues form a close bunch around him and try to force their way forward and to the near touch-line as far as they can. When the rush is stopped the ball is released and a loose scrum is formed. An alternative is to drop the ball to the ground and 'take' it forward at the feet.

2. *Inter-passing After a Break-away*

An individual forward breaks through the line-out on his own after gaining possession and is joined by his colleagues to continue the attack with close passing.

3. *Long Line-out*

The ball is thrown from touch to the player standing at the back of the line-out who then starts an attack. He is quickly joined by his colleagues or he links with the threequarters. Great accuracy in throwing is needed by the wing-threequarter.

4. *The Mobile Line-out*

(*a*) The ball is thrown to one of the forwards standing at the back of the line-out. While the ball travels through the air to the receiver the players in the forward part of the line-out turn outward and run parallel with the line toward the open side. The

receiver, after gaining possession, passes the ball to one
of the moving forwards and an attack by close inter-
passing is developed in the open ground behind the
line-out.

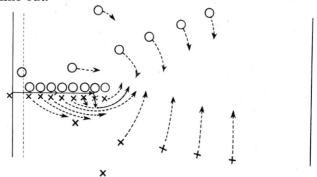

(b) Should the defending forwards take counter-
measures by also turning outward and run to cover the

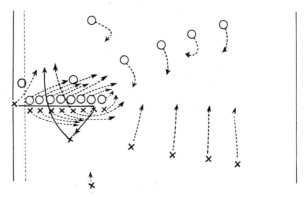

open side, the attack should then be switched to the
blind side. Instead of passing to one of the forwards
running round the line-out, the receiver should pass

directly to the scrum-half who tries to break through on the blind side.

Practices

1. Skip jumps. Emphasis on good ankle and knee extension.

2. High skip jumps. Emphasis on fast hip, knee, and ankle drive.

3. Alternate skip jumps and deep jumps. On landing after the skip jump, the knees are fully bent and are then vigorously straightened for a high vertical jump.

4. Tuck jumps.

5. Continuous vertical jumps to touch a high object with both hands.

6. Line-out practice in pairs. No. 1 lobs the ball for No. 2 to jump and catch with both hands.

7. In threes. No. 1 lobs the ball. No. 2 jumps to catch with both hands, lands, and passes to No. 3 who acts as scrum-half. Line-out player must practise to both sides.

8. As in 7. The line-out player turns in the air to land facing the scrum-half.

9. As in 8. The line-out player turns and passes before descending.

10. As in 9. Varying the methods of giving the ball to the scrum-half.

11. In fives. One thrower, two line-out players and two scrum-halves.

12. As in 11. Increasing the number of line-out players.

13. Line-out practice to bring the ball down for loose scrummaging drills. Only token opposition at first, e.g. three opponents who bind to support the heeling pack.

14. Tactical drills from the line-out.

9/*Scrummaging*

THE qualities required for good tight and loose scrummaging are weight, strength, stamina, skill, and the intelligence to use them effectively without undue waste of energy. Scrummaging is but one phase of a forward's duties, and if most of his energy is spent at it he will use line-out and open play as a means to snatch a rest. There can be no rest for forwards who faithfully fulfil their duties. They should be the fittest men in the team, especially in modern rugby, when the rules encourage them to take a greater part in open play and handling movements. If they fail to prepare and adapt themselves to these more progressive rugby ideas, then they must blame themselves for the stagnation of so many games and the loss of support from the public.

But no matter how well forwards adapt themselves to modern rugby, they must still be first and foremost good, wholehearted scrummagers, and it is only after this duty that they are expected to run and handle as modern forwards should. No one phase of play should be neglected for greater glory in another.

Binding and Packing

The foundation of the scrum is formed by the three front-row men who bind together and pack down against the opposing front row.

The middle man (hooker) raises his arms to allow his two front-row colleagues (props) to place their inside shoulders under his armpits and grip him about the body with their inside arms; the hooker then brings his own arms down over their inside shoulders and across their backs to grip with the hands just below the props' outside armpits. All three pull together to bind tightly and pack down against their opposite numbers. The props should have their backs straight and horizontal, with the outside foot forward and the inside foot placed behind and roughly in line. The rear knee should be slightly bent ready to impart the necessary forward drive at the appropriate time, while the forward leg follows the ball into the scrum to help the hooker, or to prevent the ball emerging again from the tunnel between the front rows. The line of the feet is slightly outside the centre-line of the body, so that the props lean inward toward the hooker.

Contrary to general opinion, the hooker cannot pack with a straight flat back, nor can he help appreciably in pushing if he is to place himself in the most advantageous position to manœuvre the hips and legs in hooking. Neither can he pack with his head forced back, especially if he is the tight head hooker, i.e. the hooker whose head is further away from the scrum-half when the latter puts in the ball. To be able to see the ball beyond three other heads this hooker must of necessity lower his head as far as possible without upsetting the solidity of the front-row binding. Here lies the vital need for low packing. The hooker who is lower is better able to see the ball as it leaves the scrum-half's hands, while the lower props, by forcing their opponents upwards, place the opposing hooker at a greater disadvantage. The hooker has both feet turned slightly toward the side on which the scrum-half stands with the striking foot a little in advance of the other. Both knees are bent. The best advice one could give to the hooker in packing is, to get into a position which is 'comfortable' and allows mobility of the hips and legs, to rely entirely on the props for the necessary lateral support, and concentrate his whole being on a fast strike to gain possession of the ball.

The two second-row men (the locks) bind together by wrapping their inside arms about each other's waist and pack down with their heads pushed in between the props and hooker. Their shoulders should be placed low on the buttocks of the front-row men with their outside arms around the props' hips and gripping the shorts or jersey with the hands. Most of the push will be directed by the outside shoulder against the props while the hooker is given a measure of freedom to manœuvre to strike rapidly. Their backs should be straight and flat, and eyes looking for the ball.

The position of the feet depends on the scrum formation. For the 3–2–3 form the outside foot is placed forward with the inner foot placed roughly behind it, but in the 3–4–1 formation the opposite is in favour, inside foot forward and the outside foot behind. Occasionally the second-row forward on the side on which the ball enters the scrum may choose to pack with the feet astride and parallel, leaving a tunnel for the ball between his feet. Some first-class forwards advocate this method for both second-row men, but it is unlikely to prove a more effective method than the established fore and aft foot placing.

The middle of the back-row men (No. 8) packs with head back, and back flat, between the two second-row men. His shoulders should be low against their buttocks with his arms high about their hips and pulling them inward. Both knees should be bent, feet apart and in line astride, with the toes turned outward slightly.

If the scrum formation is of the 3–2–3 type the two wing-forwards pack with their inside shoulders against the outside buttocks of the second-row pair, inside arms binding round the middle man in the back row with the outside foot forward and inside foot back. In the 3–4–1 formation they pack in similar fashion against the props, with the inside arm binding with their respective second-row men. The feet are reversed to have the inside foot forward and outside foot back.

No hard and fast rules can be laid down for foot placings in the scrum. Each pack must experiment to find the foot position best suited to its members. A scrum is a constantly moving mass, and the feet must be frequently and quickly adjusted to be in position for maximum driving power when the time comes, and to help heel the ball back should the need arise.

Loose Scrum

A loose scrum is formed when one or more players from both teams gather over the ball which is already on the ground. The subsequent binding is in no set order as in the tight scrum but it should simulate it in compactness, efficiency, and purpose. The speed in which a pack forms a loose scrum is also important.

The ball may either be driven forward at the feet of the advancing pack, wheeled and dribbled on, or heeled quickly to the backs. The first players over the ball bind to form a solid front row and the rest enter the scrum where they can contribute their weight and skill to the best advantage. Eyes must be looking for the ball and effort directed toward the tactic suggested by the forward leader. Aimless hacking, shoving, and wrestling contribute only to wasting energy.

Hooking and Heeling

Hooking is a matter of timing and the speed with which the hooking leg can be shot diagonally across the tunnel to intercept the ball and heel it back. All other things being equal, the hooker with the fastest strike should always win the ball, therefore speeding up the strike should be the hooker's aim in life and this can only be achieved through much practice.

Since the change allowing the tight head hooker to use his near foot, a greater responsibility has been placed on the props, especially the one nearer the side on which the scrum-half puts in the ball. When the far foot is used to hook, it is often necessary for the prop to give assistance with his outside foot by following the ball into the scrum, but in the new method his assistance is essential. The hooker can do little more than shoot his near leg across the tunnel to intervene between the opposing hooker's legs and the ball which is then stopped or deflected. It is then the prop's duty to bring his outside foot to the ball to heel it. The whole operation is a joint pincer movement, nicely timed, so that the prop's foot comes in contact with the ball almost at the same time as that of the hooker. Some hookers have developed a back-heeling action when hooking with the near foot. After intercepting the ball they scoop it backwards with the heel.

Pushing should not stop when the hooker heels the ball. It will reach the scrum-half quickest if, as it rolls back, the pack continues to move forward over it. The feet should be quickly and correctly adjusted either to avoid impeding its travel or to assist it on its way out. Points to remember in scrummaging are: to bind tight and pack low; flat straight backs (a good scrum is as flat as a table top); foot and leg positions which give good balance and maximum driving power; a determined and concerted shove; eyes looking for the ball.

Wheeling

This is probably best attempted when the 3–2–3 scrum formation is used. Once the hooker gains possession of the ball it should be directed to the second-row player on the side of the intended wheel. At the same time the weight of the pack is directed on the prop on that side to drive the scrum round to the opposite way. The prop on the other side either holds his ground or heaves backward pulling his opposite number with him to help the turning movement of the scrum. When the scrum has turned about 45 degrees the second-row man breaks with the ball at his feet and dribbles on. He is quickly followed by his second-row partner and the wing forward on that side, followed closely behind by the other two back-row players. The defending back-row players, once they interpret the tactic, must break quickly to check the attack either by falling on the ball or locking with the dribblers to form a loose scrum.

Practices

1. Contests.

2. Weight Training, for leg and general strength. For all players of 14 years of age and over.

3. Scrum push in pairs. Emphasis on good foot, leg and body positions.

4. Scrum push in fours. Two against two with correct arm binding, and foot placing as for second row.

5. Scrum push in sixes. Three against three. Middle man binds as hooker. Correct foot positions for the two outside players (props).

6. Scrum push in tens.

7. Scrum push in twelves.

8. As in 7 with two full packs. Emphasis on correct foot, leg, body and arm positions, with opportunity to experiment in 3–2–3, 3–4–1 and 3–3–2 scrum formations. Coach to signal the start of the pushing contest.

9. Scrum practice against scrummaging machine (if available). The main point to emphasize is the timing of the initial push when the scrum-half puts in the ball.

10. Front-row hooking practice. The elementary principles of hooking can first be practised with one front row in position against a wall or railing supported by the stretched outside arms of the props, with the coach or scrum-half to put in the ball. Hooking with both the far and the near foot should be practised and teamwork between the hooker and the props is essential when hooking with the near foot.

11. As in 10, with two front rows packing against each other but only one set practising at a time.

12. As in 11, both hookers striking for possession.

13. Two full packs. Hooking and heeling practice.

14. One full pack opposed by three front-row forwards. The full pack heel the ball to the second or third row and advance with the ball at the feet. Later this activity can be done near the try line to practise the push over try.

15. Players arranged as in 14. Wheeling practice.

16. As in 15 with two full packs.

17. As in 16, but as soon as the wheel begins the defending wing-forward on that side detaches himself from the scrum and falls on the ball.

18. As in 17 followed by a loose scrum.

19. Set scrum. Forwards break from the scrum in defence and corner flag.

20. Set scrum. Forwards break from the scrum and follow an imaginary attack by their threequarters.

Loose Scrummaging

1. Forwards arranged in two groups standing a few yards apart. On a signal both groups walk forward and form a loose scrum. The first players up form the front row irrespective of their normal positions in the set scrum. Emphasis on good binding and packing.

2. As in 1, but as the groups meet, the coach throws the ball on the ground between them and they compete to gain possession of the ball.

3. Both groups trot up and form a loose scrum over the ball, which is already on the ground and try to heel.

4. As in 3 at speed.

5. Both groups stand a few yards apart. On a signal they walk to form a loose scrum over a player already lying on the ground alongside the ball. The first two or three players from one group in turn are allowed to step over the lying player to get between the ball and the opponents and thus gain an advantage. In the early stages of this practice the players could be allowed to wear gym shoes.

6. As in 5, players run to form the scrum and compete for possession.

7. Two groups facing each other 10–15 yards apart. One group (attackers) dribble the ball slowly toward the defenders. One defender falls on the ball and a loose scrum is formed.

8. Wheeling practice from a loose scrum.

9. Players practise breaking to attack and defence positions from a loose scrum. In the loose scrum players

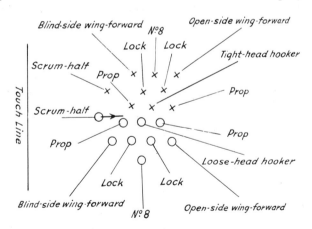

normally in the front or second row of the set scrum might occasionally be the players most conveniently placed to play the wing-forward part in the ensuing open play.

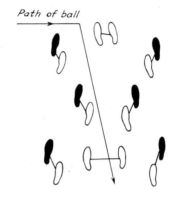

Position of feet in 3–2–3 scrum formation

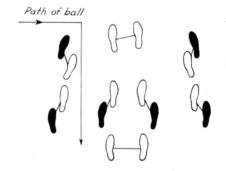

Position of feet in 3–4–1 scrum formation

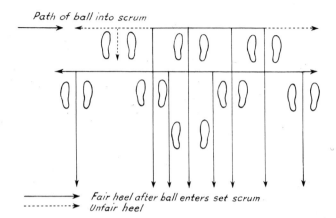

Path of ball into scrum

Fair heel after ball enters set scrum
Unfair heel

High up in the line-out

The scrum

10 / The Coach

THE duty of the coach is to provide a system of training which will give players a comprehensive preparation for playing rugby; to help them in their mental and physical approach to become better players; and to show them how to combine their efforts so that a higher standard of play can be achieved.

His work must be designed to cover all aspects of the game, and he must ensure that these improve together, as far as possible, so that the full effect of one is not hampered by the lack of another. One has only to think of the player who beats his man with a perfect side-step only to be caught from behind by the same defender because of lack of speed, or of the failure of the player with a good burst of speed, who lacks the stamina to maintain it for more than a short distance, to realize the importance of an all-round training.

If players are to receive the full benefit of this type of training, the coach must have a thorough understanding of the game, its skills, tactics and methods of training. He needs to gain the confidence and respect of the players right from the beginning. His enthusiasm should permeate through the team, so that the players enjoy even serious training. The coach should try to be impartial: often strict yet sometimes sympathetic: frequently generous with praise for good work and effort, especially to young players. He must be careful not to overdo a particular phase of training, yet give the players sufficient to leave them with a feeling that the work was worth while and beneficial. Even the best players have some fault or other, and good coaching will help iron it out. The more faults a player has the more he should benefit from coaching. Some faults may be in the technical application of the skills and others will concern tactics. Many are easily seen but to eliminate them is often much more difficult. *Above all the coach must be able to see faults and know how to eliminate them.*

It would obviously be foolhardy to bring faults to a player's notice without some constructive advice. A player gets too much of that as it is. He probably realizes his mistakes and wishes that he did not make them. What he needs more than anything is sympathy and encouragement and to be shown how to correct his faults.

A diffident approach to coaching will never get the best out of players. The coach must know exactly what he aims to do and how to set about achieving it and his training sessions must be well prepared beforehand. The type of tactical training, for instance, will probably be based on the faults seen in the last game. He must be the 'expert' and win the respect of the players as such.

It is important to recognize potential ability. A great number of players have never risen above the average class because of the lack of coaching, or the failure of the coach to develop latent ability. An all-round training and a few words of advice can often change players from average to good. A player in one position may have one or two bad faults which are difficult to correct, but his good qualities may be put to better use in another position. Average club players have been known to become internationals in this way.

The approach to the coaching of young schoolboys will differ from that of ordinary club coaching. The interest of club players in rugby is well established. Young schoolboys have still to decide. The boys will need to be given a happy introduction to rugby and the way in which the coach tackles the job will have a profound effect on the future attitude of many of the boys toward rugby and training. The diffident and less robust boys will need particular attention, and will require shrewd handling and coaching if they are not to be lost to rugby at an early age. It is fairly easy to coach a group of boys whose ability and eagerness are roughly the same, but individual ability in a normal group of thirty to forty boys will vary appreciably. The better boys must not be expected to practise all the time the same simple skills as the poor ones if they are to progress at the rate which their aptitude would allow, and to expect the poor players to keep up with the good ones will only result in failure and further lack of confidence. Indeed the coaching at this stage must be based on common sense principles of teaching.

The problem of arranging a training schedule is quite easy if the coach bears in mind that the needs of the players are more stamina, speed, agility, skill in the basic arts, and tactical ability and knowledge. A good training session should include activities to maintain and improve all these components of rugby. If the session is to be of one and a half hour's duration then the schedule for a senior club could be arranged like this:

Stamina—before and early season 15–20 mins.
Speed and Agility   20 mins.
Skills   20 mins.
Tactics   20–30 mins.
Game, e.g. touch rugby,
   seven-a-side   10–15 mins.

The activities to include can be taken from the chapter under each of the headings, the time distribution being modified at the discretion of the coach. For schoolboys the coach should take into account the age and ability of the boys. With very young players the main concern is to get them to like rugby and improve the skills. Later when they become proficient handlers and can play a game fairly well, then training for stamina, speed, evading etc., must be included to improve the general standard of play.

11 / Speed

A RUGBY player probably does more running than anything else during a game, and therefore it should receive as much attention in the training session as some
of the other arts. Good style in particular should be
sought in the early stages. Good style means economical
running, which in turn means greater staying power,
while in poor style many superfluous movements
take place, thus hampering speed and wasting
energy.

Players who want speed must be prepared to tackle
the job of acquiring it with the same sense of purpose as
an athlete, and should be prepared to spend much time
at it in the summer months as well as during the rugby
season. It is wise for every rugby player to join an
athletic club and practise with athletes to keep fit and
develop speed between the seasons. It is easier to keep
fit than to get fit, and by keeping fit the player may
lengthen his career. Far too many good players retire
prematurely because they have forgotten this.

Points to remember in developing style are: to
point the feet in the direction of the run, the knees
moving forward, upward, and slightly inward. The arm
action should be forward and backward with the forward hand moving across to the centre line of the
body—no further—at shoulder height. Too much, or

insufficient force in the arm action will hamper good body balance.

Correct body angle (slight forward lean) should be aimed for in technique, with a good high knee lift, together with a strong downward and backward drive of the legs and a good length stride. With regard to length of stride, there seems to be a key distance in every individual's sprinting stride which will help to give maximum speed. A leg action which is too fast usually means short stride lengths, while running strides which are too long mean a too slow leg action. In between is the key position, that is, a stride length and leg speed which makes the most effective contribution to speed. Of course this is not the sole requirement for speed, but it is an important part of sprinting technique which will help individuals to develop greater pace. To find this key stride it may be necessary for players to experiment in timed sprint starts of 15–20 strides, preferably with the supervision of a qualified athletic coach.

Running with the ball puts one or both arms out of action as aids to balance and speed, so that a slight adjustment in technique will be required. This is usually achieved through the various passing practices at speed.

Speed in rugby is often being adjusted to meet the continuously changing situations, and the nicety of the adjustments will depend upon the players' ability to judge the distance and the speed of the play around him. The extra man cannot make any effective contributions to the attack if he does not possess the ability to judge distance and speed.

It will often be necessary to increase and decrease

speed and to change direction very quickly, either in attack or defence. Rugby then, needs control in running, and controlled running ensures mobility. Controlled speed means being able to reach maximum speed very quickly and to stop again even quicker, and being able to vary the pace to execute smoothly the various evading tactics. The faster one runs, the more difficult it is to change direction. A quick change of pace to a slower speed may be necessary; strides are shortened, and there is a shift in body weight to change momentum from one direction to another. Often this must be done within a very few yards. Therefore, being able to stop quickly in rugby is as important as being able to reach top speed very quickly. A quick stop will often cause the defender to over-run the attacker, with obvious repercussions. It is often preceded by an acceleration to get the defender to move fast.

Acceleration, as we associate it with rugby, is an explosive burst of speed from a stationary position, or a slow rate, to top speed in the minimum possible distance. To see a player beat his man on the outside by sheer acceleration is one of the delights of rugby: to do it is even better. A preceding change of pace to a slower speed slows down the opponent. It is obviously harder and demands more effort to reach top speed quickly from a stationary position than it does when the player is already moving. It is therefore essential that plenty of sprint starts should be included in the training. To 'warm up' for these, there should be several bursts from slow to top speed, sprinkled generously with quick stopping and starting practices. Sprinting practice during the season should more often than not be done in boots on grass rather than in spikes on a track. Sprint starts should be mostly from a standing position, because this more nearly approximates to the conditions of the game. A little sprint training, if at all possible, should be done every day to keep the edge on speed, especially in the first 10–15 strides. Competitive training stimulates interest and effort.

The fact that it quickens reactions supports the need for bouts of fast work in rugby training. This is important because the movements of the players in one team are influenced by the position of the ball and of the opponents. Players who can react faster to the changing situations and the movements of the ball, and who can start off faster in a sprint and be in the right place at the right time, have a definite advantage over those who react slowly. Fatigue usually slows down reaction time.

Weight Training for Speed

The only way to develop more power is to exercise the muscles against progressively increasing resistance, and the most effective way is with the use of barbells and weights. Weight training of the right kind makes a definite contribution to the development of speed, but it must be remembered that weight training alone is not the whole answer. It is an adjunct, but a necessary one, to the speed training and the improved sprinting technique. Weight training, systematically and sensibly conducted, will not only develop strength but also greater flexibility in the joints.

For further information and activities the reader is recommended to the books *Basic Weight Training*,

Weight Training for Sport and Fitness, *Weight Training for Athletics*.

Speed Training Practices

1. *Running on the Spot.* Emphasis on a very high knee action. Later speed up to as fast as possible.

2. *Fast Walking.* Emphasis on very fast leg movements and short strides using the arms as in running.

3. *Sprinting on the Spot.* Emphasis on fast leg action.

4. *Bounding.* Running with long strides emphasising the rear leg drive.

5. *Bounding up Stairs.* Two, three, or four at a time.

6. *Sprinting up Sloping Ground.*

7. *Trot and Burst.* Trot for a shorter distance then burst to top speed on signal. In groups of three or four.

8. *Sprint Starts.* Sprint for 50 yards in groups of three or four for competition. Crouch starts.

9. *Sprint Starts.* From standing starts in threes or fours for competition.

10. *Sprint–Stop–Accelerate.* Top-speed sprint for a short distance—stop quickly on signal—accelerate on second signal. Repeat several times.

11. *Sprint–Turn–Accelerate.* Top-speed sprint for a short distance—stop, turn about and accelerate on signal. Repeat several times.

12 / Stamina

APPLIED to the game stamina is the physical ability of the player to play high-pressure rugby from beginning to end without undue signs of fatigue, loss of form, and speed. To possess stamina will be a distinct advantage, and without it a player will rarely rise above mediocrity. To get it necessitates self-discipline and hard training, especially before and at the beginning of the season. Later in the season there could be less emphasis on developing stamina and more concentration on skill, tactics and speed training. These in themselves will at least maintain stamina provided the training is well organised and conducted at a brisk pace.

Lack of stamina will result in early fatigue with the accompanying loss of form and speed; mental and physical reactions are slowed down and play becomes erratic and inefficient.

The only way to develop stamina is to indulge in prolonged physical activity of gradually increasing intensity, and involving the use of the whole body. This means running, running and still more running, gradually increasing the distance, or speed, or both, if real fitness is to be achieved. There must always be an increase in the intensity of the work if stamina is to be developed. When training slackens or stops, the player then begins gradually to lose the strength, stamina and speed which he developed during the training.

For decades lapping round the pitch has been the popular 'stint' of rugby players in developing stamina. If this method is to be used, then the running must be of good pace and maintained for 20 minutes or so. In this time the runner should have covered a distance of about three miles. A few laps at a slow pace twice a week will be of little or no value. *Far too many players still play rugby to keep fit instead of getting fit to play rugby*. The aim should be to develop stamina in excess of the demand made during the game.

Obviously this should not be attempted at the beginning of the training for the new season, after the summer lay off. To plunge immediately into a strenuous programme of training would be asking for trouble and indeed actually delay the attainment of peak fitness. Untrained muscles may be stretched and torn, necessitating a rest for a week or so to enable them to recover before training can be resumed.

A common-sense approach, then, must be adopted toward early training and there must be a gradual ascent to full effort. To begin with, alternately walking at a crisp pace and trotting four or five times round the pitch should suffice, but the training session should continue with some stationary passing practice with emphasis on speed and accuracy of passes. Progress should then be made to continuous running, and as endurance develops so should the speed and number of laps. This training should continue for about twenty minutes at a good speed if any benefit is to be derived from it and it should be remembered that during a full training session the stamina training should take up only one-quarter or one-fifth of the time. The rest of the time should be devoted to speed, skills, tactics and possibly a game of touch rugby at the end.

Some players may shun the monotony of lapping and would seek a variant in the training. Road or cross country running may prove to them a more interesting way of developing rugby fitness, especially if a little variety is put into the running. Clubs whose head-quarters are within easy reach of large parks or common land have a definite advantage. After a few evenings of easy runs to strengthen the muscles generally, the running could then be increased and varied, switching from the normal long-distance trot to include an occasional prolonged run for 400 to 500 yards followed by brisk walks until breathing has returned to near normal and then frequent bursts of speed for 50 to 100 yards. Steeply sloping ground should not be avoided. Sharp sprints up these will help to get extra strength and drive in the legs for speed.

The ball should be taken on these runs. Many teams neglect the use of the ball in early training until players feel fit enough to embark on some fast passing practice. This is wrong. The ball should never be excluded from any training session. Bouts of interpassing should take place during the runs, and an occasional unexpected kick ahead and sprint to be the first man to the ball will add to the interest of the training. Just for the fun of it, a cross-country race could be organised occasionally and it will help to bring out that extra bit of effort.

Another form of stamina training is a modified form of the system of 'interval running' used by many first-class middle- and long-distance runners. This involves running a set distance—say once round the pitch—in a given time, followed by a short rest, and repeating the procedure until the runner feels adequately trained. For example, one lap of the pitch in 60 seconds followed by 60 to 90 seconds rest, repeated several times. Further development is achieved by increasing the speed and number of laps and diminishing the rest time between each lap.

The old favourite—walk–trot–sprint up and down the field—still has its place in rugby training provided the practice is prolonged and increased gradually to maximum effort.

Some players may be so fit that they can afford to do less stamina training than others, but no player is so fit that he can ignore it completely.

13/*Agility*

AGILITY in games is essential if the player aims to rise above the average. To be quick in everything one does, is to have a definite advantage over slower-moving colleagues. All players need agility, but in particular the scrum-half. He must be here, there and everywhere and his special duties require him to be stooping and crouching and moving about very quickly in a low position, one minute running, next minute on the ground and then up again in a flash to carry on the play. Forwards need it so that they can stoop quickly to pick up a loose ball and start a passing movement before a loose scrum has time to form. Backs who are half-tackled and bowled over, must be agile enough to roll and be up on the feet to continue the attack before the defence recovers. Some players fail to produce the quick movement of a pass when falling, or a full-back cannot field a rolling ball because he is too stiff to stoop and gather! To be agile requires practice in activities which need strong, quick movements of the whole body, and, where pace over the ground is also involved, there should be a deliberate effort to develop more and more speed.

Practising gymnastics is an excellent way of promoting agility because they demand fast strong explosive movements involving the whole body weight.

Other practices include:

1. Scoring runs. Two parallel lines not more than
10 yards apart. The players stand behind one line A and
on a signal they race across to touch-line B and back a
set number of times, or as many times as they can in a
given time, say 20 seconds. The runners must touch the
lines with the hand. The first player home is the winner.

2. Change the balls practice. Three lines are drawn
(or three markers) 5 yards apart with a ball placed on
lines A and C. The player starts from behind line A
and runs to pick up the ball and places it on line B. He
continues to run to line C., to pick up the second ball,
and returns to place it on line A, and so on. He handles
each ball in turn and places it on the vacant line (or
marker) trying to keep up the practice at high speed.

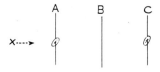

3. Potato Race. Teams of four. Four, five or six balls,
or other objects, arranged as in diagram. No. 1 runs to

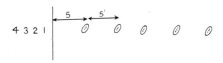

collect one ball, and places it behind the starting line, he then runs for the next one and so on until all have been collected. No. 2 replaces them in the same way. No. 3 collects, No. 4 replaces.

4. Under and over canes. 18 inches to 2 feet high and 2 yards apart. Players in teams of four. Rows of about six canes placed horizontally on skittles etc. Players alternately jump over and scramble under the canes. Nos. 1 and 3 stand at one end of the row, Nos. 2 and 4 at the other end. No. 1 runs under and over to touch off No. 2. No. 2 then runs to touch No. 3, and so on until all have had their turn.

14/*Tactics*

TACTICS are team manœuvres and plans of campaign designed to defeat the opposition. Variety in play and success in the match will depend entirely on the skill and morale of the players.

If the players lack the necessary skill in the arts of rugby then many very useful tactics cannot be employed or, if attempted, they invariably fail. A three-quarter line cannot use quick passing as a tactic to beat the defence if they are not capable of passing quickly enough; forwards cannot use short passing as a variation of tactics if they cannot handle well enough in a confined space against a close defence, and unorthodox tactics will fail if players lack the ability to time their passes to a split second, lack the judgement to join the moves at the precise moment, and do not possess the speed and determination to carry them through to a successful conclusion. Hence the vital importance of practising the basic skills, not only in isolation but under game conditions, for without a high standard of proficiency in them the success and variety of tactics will be very limited.

Many tactics involve the combined understanding and co-operation of two, three or more players and to use them with effect requires much thought and collective practice. The development of a tactic follows the same process as learning a skill. At first the manœuvre needs thought, and every detail of its pattern must be understood. Then it must be practised unopposed, slowly, and with deliberation so that the players become accustomed to the directional running and timing without interference from opponents. Eventually, with continued practice, it will be possible, quite spontaneously, to execute the tactic with skill and fluency almost in the nature of a reflex action. Once this stage has been reached, 'token' opposition should then be introduced to test its accuracy, timing, and speed, and gradually more and more opponents should be brought in until they equal the number of attackers. It is very important in the early stages to practise a tactic without opponents so that a quick success in it is achieved and that players develop confidence in their ability to use it.

The opposing players in tactical training should be members of the 'A' team, for in this way they will be practising with players of superior skill and learning the tactics employed by the first team, so that when the time comes for their promotion they will know the various moves in which they will be expected to take part. This will help to lessen the disorganisation which usually results from the introduction of a new player to a team. The guiding principles of team tactics are:

1. To establish a moral supremacy right from the start. This means getting on top early by adopting tactics in both attack and defence which disconcert and demoralise the opponents before they settle down to any set pattern of play.

2. To maintain high-pressure play and harass the

opponents continuously. Once supremacy has been gained there must be no 'letting up' or complacency. An all-out effort must be maintained to keep the initiative and to further wear down the opponents.

3. To gain possession, keep possession and attack. These speak for themselves. There is nothing more disheartening to a forward who has toiled in the scrum for the ball than to see it being frittered away by unnecessary kicking and poor handling by the backs. Once the ball is in possession every effort should be made to keep and use it to attack in true rugby fashion.

4. To back-up. Good backing-up is one of the most effective 'tactics' in rugby. If every player backs-up intelligently and places himself in a position to carry on the play there is very little the opponents can do to stop such attacks.

5. To detect and exploit the opponents' weaknesses. By probing attacks and variation of tactics certain weaknesses in the opponents' defences may be discovered, and once they are known, they must be exploited by throwing the full weight of the attack on to them. If, through previous experience, a weakness in the opponents' team is known beforehand, then early tactics must be designed to break through at that point in the hope that an advantage can be gained before the defenders settle upon counter-measures to cover up the weakness.

6. To make full use of the team's strength and cover up the weaknesses. Many teams are stronger in some positions and aspects of play than in others and these factors will, to a large extent, determine the tactics to be used. If the team is particularly strong at

three-quarter, the forwards should feed them the ball as quickly and as often as possible. If however the backs are weak and ineffective against a sound defence, then the forwards should retain the ball whenever possible and employ wheels, dribbles, and close passing to make the initial breaks, so that the backs will link up and use their speed to finish off the moves.

7. To adapt play to meet the present conditions. Poor weather conditions generally means kick and rush tactics and little or no handling, and the main reason for adopting them is the inability of the players to handle a greasy ball. Obviously a muddy ground and a wet ball are bound to hamper open play. The handicap could be largely overcome if players would only prac-tise handling in bad conditions instead of cancelling training sessions when the weather is unfavourable. Evasive tactics should also be practised so that players develop the confidence to use them during a game. A slippery ground can be used to advantage by the attacker. He has the initiative and therefore a little more time to gather himself to execute his plan cor-rectly. The defender will find it at least difficult on such a surface to change his direction or pace quickly enough to counter. Another good reason why the backs should be more in the play is that cold and wet weather some-times adversely affects the standard of tackling among backs who have been inactive for long periods of the game. This is the time when really determined running brings results.

Strong winds will affect the kicking tactics and the positional play of some of the players. When playing with a strong wind the full-back will stand closer to the play, and should use the wind to gain ground with his touch kicking, but when playing against a strong wind, he, and the two wings, will stand further behind the play, keep his kicks low and make sure of finding touch at the expense of distance. Kicking generally should be kept to a minimum.

Other examples of adjusting tactics to meet the needs of the situation include:

Abandoning tactics which prove ineffective and trying others; positional changes when a player is injured; removing an off-form player to a less vital position; stalling tactics to rest a tired pack (unnecessary if players are fit); and testing untried moves near the end of the game when leading by a safe margin of points.

8. To vary play, change the direction of the attack and use unorthodox surprise moves. Team tactics should vary continuously during a game so that opponents are unable to anticipate moves and are constantly kept in a state of uncertainty.

A scrum-half who never veers from his primary duty of passing to the fly-half makes it increasingly difficult for the latter to evade his opposite number and the wing forward, who are able to anticipate the scrum-half's play and gain vital yards in defensive covering. Threequarters who always try to beat their men on the outside and who rely upon individual players to make openings, instead of combining their efforts to vary the form of attacks, make defensive play easy for the opponents. The aim is to know, and use, a variety of tactics which confuse the defenders and reduce them to a state of not knowing what to do for the best.

A quick change in the direction of the attack is one of

the best methods of putting defenders out of position, and to take full advantage of this move it is important that players position themselves correctly. It is simply a case of using one form of attack as a decoy to weaken the defence in the area of the main attack and then throwing the full weight of the attack on to that point. One of the most elementary ways of doing this is to pass the ball along the threequarter line to the wing on one side of the field, and if he finds his way forward barred, he gives an inside pass to a supporting player who starts a passing movement to the opposite side; by this time the rest of the team should be in line formation across the field just behind the ball ready to back up in the new direction. Inside passes and 'scissors' movements should be used to start new attacks from any position on the field.

Unorthodox play is the term given to tactics which involve the use of reverse passes, dummy reverse passes, 'scissors' movements, using an extra man, and various moves other than the conventional threequarter passing movements to the wings, such as an individual player trying to defeat his opposite number with one of the basic evading skills.

The extra man, e.g. the full-back, coming up in attack, may have the opportunity of making a clear-cut break. He should certainly never join a movement merely as a link which will only delay the ball reaching the wing. Often his function will be to draw one of the opposition, and so provide an overlap or give the next receiver the opportunity of a break through the gap which has been created. Speed and determined running are very important for the extra man.

Many teams avoid the use of unorthodox and surprise tactics until near the end of a game, and then, only if a good lead in points has been built up. It seems that players feel, under these conditions, they can risk trying something out of the ordinary and that if mistakes are made they have sufficient points in hand to save the game. This defeats the purpose of their use, and, is an admission of lack of confidence, skill and practice in the moves. Unorthodox tactics were evolved primarily to outwit the defenders and produce points, and the fact that they make for more enjoyable play for the players and better entertainment value for the public is quite incidental. If supremacy is to be gained early and providing the moves have been well practised, then they should be put into use soon after the beginning of the game. At best, points will accrue; at worst, the moves will unsettle the defenders. In short, well known and practised moves should be used early, new and untried tactics should be tested near the end of a game when the team has a good lead.

Almost clear away

Over for a good try

15/*Full-back*

FULL-BACKS are often classified into types like 'safe', 'spectacular', 'kickers' or 'tacklers', each term signifying a particularly strong aspect of play in each full-back's general make-up. The 'safe' full-back is the one who never relies on chance, makes sure of his touch finding, usually at the expense of distance, and is always sound in everything he does in an unpretentious way. The 'spectacular' player has a more adventurous approach to his play, is prepared to take risks to try the un-expected, and usually makes a few mistakes in the at-tempt, but adds colour and enterprise to the general play. The 'kickers' are so called because of their prodigious and accurate touch and place kicking but possess only average ability in other aspects of full-back play, while the 'tacklers' are particularly noted for their defensive qualities.

The ideal full-back is a combination of all the types and therefore cannot be classified because he possesses ALL the necessary qualities for this position. This should be the aim of every full-back. He must never neglect the weak points in his play for greater proficiency in others; on the contrary he should give more time to practising them. One of the first requirements of a full-back is the temperament for the job. It is a lonely position. The mistakes which will inevitably occur from time to time are easily seen, and unless the full-back has the ability to retain his composure and concentrate on the immediate play and not worry about his mistakes, he will fail.

Positional play—being in the right place at the right time—and anticipation, will develop with experience, helped by concentrating on the ball and the movements of players nearest it. He must never be still, but always moving sideways or forward and backward with the movements of the ball. A slight precautionary adjustment of position early might very well save a rush to get to the ball at the last minute. This is the time when most mistakes are made; the full-back's efforts may become so hurried that they lack style and control. The full-back must be reliable and give his colleagues a feeling of confidence in his ability to do the right things.

He must be a good catcher under all conditions and have the ability to punt well with either foot. In addition he must be one of the best place and drop kickers in the team, and he must never cease to practise the arts. His tackling and ability to fall and stop foot rushes must be unquestionable. He must never fail to take the opportunity of turning defence into attack. The full-back who always kicks to touch after receiving is unimaginative and lacks enterprise. His contribution to attacking play generally must be adventurous and timely. The full-back has always been described as the last line of defence, which of course he is, but it must be noted, only when the opponents have the ball. Rarely, if ever, is he described as the spearhead of the attack which he must often be if an extra man is required in the attack to penetrate a good defence He is better placed, than any other player to do this. He is behind the play and has a good over-all picture of what goes on, and from such a position he has an excellent opportunity of joining the attack in the right place at the right time. Furthermore, his running will be more in a direct line up-field than that of any other player who makes the extra man. When threequarter play reaches stalemate individual players being unable to elude their opposite numbers and defence being equal to attack, then something unorthodox must be tried in order to break through. The obvious way is to increase the number of attackers by introducing an extra man, and who better than the full-back. How deep the full-back positions himself therefore depends on his reading of the play and this can only be learned by experience in match play.

Attacking Practices

1. *Catch and Counter-attack.* Full-back and three other players. No. 1 standing about 25 yards away, kicks the ball to the full-back and follows up to challenge him. The full-back makes his catch and runs slightly diagonally to link up with Nos. 2 and 3, who, acting as fly-half and centre should drop back to assist the full-back when they see No. 1 kick.

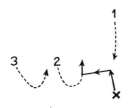

2. *Catch, Evade and Counter-attack*. As in 1 but the full-back evades No. 1 using side-step, and swerve or hand-off and runs to link with Nos. 2 and 3.

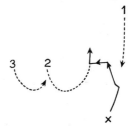

3. As in 1 and 2, with two or three follow-up players converging on the full-back.

4. As in 1, 2, and 3, but No. 1 kicks the ball along the ground.

Tactics in Attack

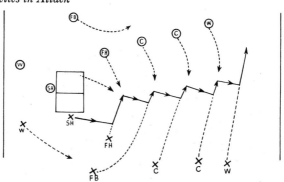

1. The full-back joins the attack between the fly-half and the inside-centre and draws the opposing inside-centre to make an overlap on the right wing. He could also join inside the fly-half, between the centres and between the centre and wing.

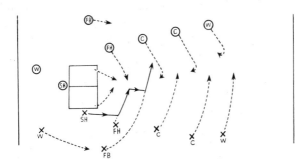

2. The full-back takes a short pass from the fly-half and makes a clear-cut opening between the opposing fly-half and inside-centre. The fly-half must run well up to the opposition and the inside-centre could attract the attention of his opposite number by calling for the ball.

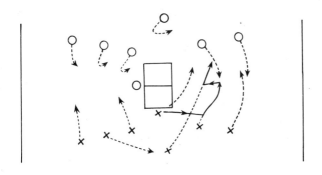

3. The fly-half runs to attract attention on the open side. The scrum-half passes to the centre on the blind side who draws his man and gives an inside pass to the full-back. He is backed up by the blind-side wing-forward and wing.

133

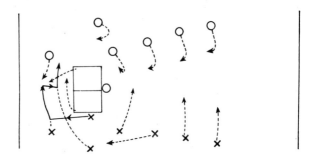

4. The scrum-half passes to the blind-side wing who runs to draw his opposite number and the blind-side wing-forward. He then gives an inside pass to the full-back. Blind-side wing-forward backs up on the inside.

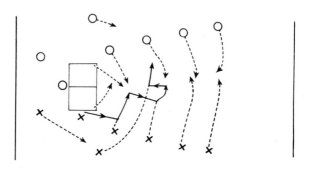

5. The fly-half runs to draw his opposite number and wing-forward. He passes to the inside-centre who immediately gives an inside pass to the full-back.

6. The scrum-half passes to the fly-half who immediately passes to the inside-centre, and then runs round the centre as if to make an extra man. The inside-centre takes a pace or two forward and inward toward the scrum and turns inward to present his back to the

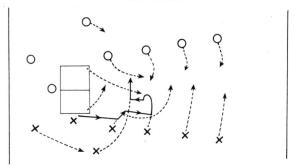

opposition, as if to give the ball to the fly-half as he runs very close round the centre. The centre in fact dummies a pass to the fly-half and then passes inside to the full-back who must run straight and hard.

By taking a few short paces forward and inward, the centre makes it easier for the fly-half to move outside him. This move is best used against a flat defence.

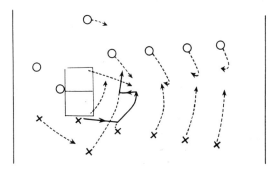

7. The scrum-half passes to the fly-half who runs diagonally for a very short distance to draw the opposition outward, then straightens his run and gives an inside pass to the full-back. This works well against a quick-breaking wing-forward and a flat defence.

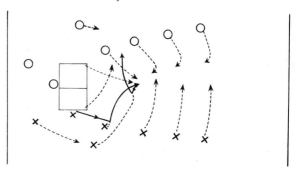

8. Just after receiving the ball the fly-half veers outward to draw the defence. At first the full-back runs parallel with the fly-half as if to make the extra man between him and the inside-centre, but at the opportune moment he changes direction inward to take the reverse pass from the fly-half. The open-side wing-forward should be in position to back up.

16/*Wing-threequarter*

In attack wings are expected to be the fastest men in the team and the leading try scorers. Speed, of course, is of considerable importance but no wing is completely equipped for the position without all-round rugby skill, determination and enterprise. In short he must be far more than just a catcher and runner and he must take full advantage of the slightest chance given to him by his centre. He should train himself to be a centre playing in the wing position so that he can create openings for himself and rely less on the centres to create them for him. Most wings expect too much of the centres and do not realize how difficult it is in modern rugby to produce the perfect situation where the wing has only to catch the ball and sprint for the line. Wings therefore are recommended to practise and play an occasional game in the centre position to appreciate the difficulties, and it will also develop their confidence to take a more active part in the attacks, especially in making the extra man from the blind-side wing position. The wing must be prepared to look for work. He should not be content to be a passive on-looker if he is deprived of the chances to attack. If the ball does not come his way then he must go to the ball and use his speed when and where he can. He should have the initiative and enterprise to pop up in the most unusual places to help further an attack, particularly when a mid-field player has broken through the defence unexpectedly and is looking for support. A wing who is able to anticipate and back up such moves adds greatly to the power of his team's attack.

A wing is expected at all times to run for the line with all the speed and determination he can muster, but if, after running some distance, he is confronted by more defenders than he can evade and he is certain to be tackled, he will merely be wasting his energy by going on. His first concern now is to keep the ball in play and in his team's possession. Two courses are open to him: he must pass inside to a supporting player or suddenly cut inside to change the direction of the attack. If the attackers back up intelligently there will always be a man in position to receive the wing's inside pass.

The cross kick is another alternative open to the wing. Ideally, the ball should be kicked across the field and forward to an open space for one of the supporting players to catch on the full volley and continue the attack by handling. This demands great accuracy in kicking, a quality seldom achieved. Therefore the cross kick should be used only as a last resort because of the risk of losing possession of the ball.

It is the wing's duty to throw the ball into the line-out from touch. Whether he uses the two-handed lobbed pass, the over-arm throw, or the American football type of one-handed throw, does not matter a great deal. The important thing as far as the wing is concerned is that the ball is thrown with great accuracy, and accuracy will improve with practice. Before he makes the throw the wing should look to the scrum-half, or forward leader, for any prearranged signal which will tell him to which forward the ball should be thrown. If no signal is given he will throw the ball to the part of the line-out opposite to where the scrum-half stands, or to an unmarked forward. A great understanding between all the players concerned in the line-out is as important as in any other form of play and this can only be developed effectively by combined practice in the training sessions.

In defence a good crash tackle on an opponent just as he is receiving the ball early in the game gives a player the same stimulus as a good attacking run, and it might have the effect of unsettling the opponent for the rest of the game. This should be the wing's first aim in defence.

If the opponents attack with an orthodox passing movement the wing should keep well up in alignment

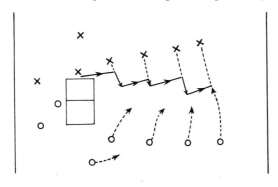

with the centres, and when he sees that the opposing outside-centre is about to pass, he accelerates to tackle his man just as he receives the ball. If the run-in is determined and well timed there is little that the opposing wing can do to avoid the tackle for he will be looking at the ball.

Another method open to the wing to bring an attack to an abrupt end is to tackle the outside-centre in the same way. This is best attempted when the defending backs stand in a more shallow alignment before the attack starts.

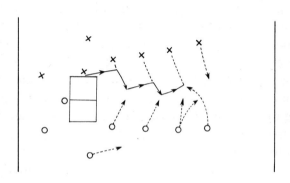

The wing will often be required to stand well back in defence to cover a possible kick ahead in his direc-

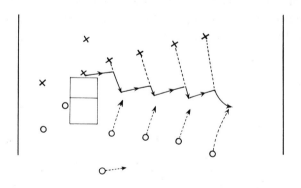

tion, and then race forward to defend against an orthodox passing movement. The wing's objective now is to
manœuvre his opponent outward to the touch-line by
keeping just far enough infield to prevent a break inside,
yet near enough to the opponent's line of approach to
make the tackle should he try to make a dash for it on
the outside.

When the opponents begin an attack on the open
side, the defending blind-side wing should automatically
move across to the middle of the field as a precautionary
measure to cover a possible unexpected break through
by a mid-field player, and he should be prepared to run
across to the opposite touch-line to help in the defence
should the need arise. It is not unusual for a blind-side
wing to bring off a try-saving tackle near the open-side
touch-line. He must also be prepared to drop back to
help the full-back. His presence there might encourage
the latter to adopt a more adventurous attitude toward
turning defence into attack.

If the wing is confronted with two attackers, e.g. a
centre with the ball and his own wing, he should always
go for the man with the ball, unless: (a) The cover
defence is near enough to tackle the centre, in which
case the wing will shadow his man.

(*b*) He can approach diagonally and shepherd them both toward the touch-line, make the centre pass to the wing and then tackle the wing.

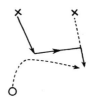

Tactics in Attack

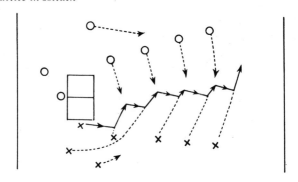

1. The blind-side wing joins the attack to make the extra man between the fly-half and centre and draws the opposing inside-centre therefore making the overlap for the open-side wing. He should begin to move into position when the ball is in the scrum. The blind-side wing could also join inside the fly-half in which case he would draw the opposing fly-half and open-side wing-forward.

2. The fly-half takes his pass and runs diagonally outward to draw the defence away from the scrum. He

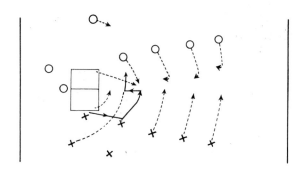

straightens his run just before the inside pass to the wing. The wing should time his run to a nicety. He must run at top speed and with great determination.

3. The wing defeats his opposite number and the full-back by using the outside swerve. He checks both defenders by straightening his run before swerving outward.

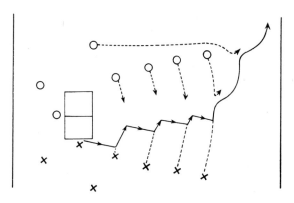

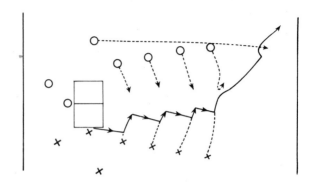

4. The wing evades the first defender with an outside swerve and continues outward toward the touch-line to encourage the full-back to maintain his speed. At the precise moment the wing side-steps inward to evade the full-back, but veers outward immediately to keep clear of the covering defence.

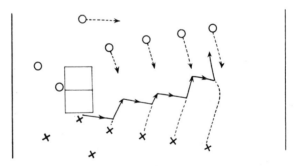

5. The wing defeats his opposite number by using the straight burst inside his man. He must be sure to straighten his run only just before he receives the ball because he must conceal his intention by moving in a diagonal path until the last moment.

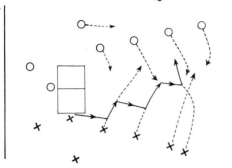

6. At first the wing runs parallel with his centre for a short distance. He then cuts inward behind the outside-centre to take a pass from the inside-centre, and makes an opening between the two opposing centres by using the straight burst. It is important that the inside-centre draws his opposite number almost to the point of being tackled and he must not 'telegraph' his pass.

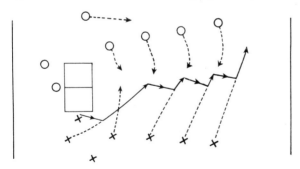

7. The fly-half runs rather straight and calls for a pass from the scrum-half. The blind-side wing moves to the open side, takes the scrum-half's pass and crosses behind the fly-half to draw the opposing inside-centre thus making an overlap for the open-side wing.

There are two other possibilities:

(*a*) The wing breaks through between the opposing fly-half and inside-centre.

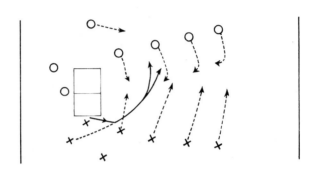

(*b*) The wing draws the opposing inside-centre to make the half opening for his own inside-centre.

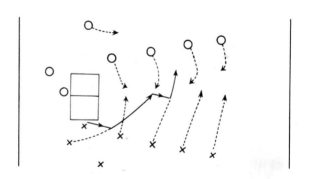

All three moves can be used with effect against a flat defence.

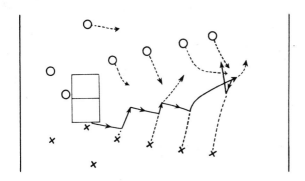

8. The open-side wing takes a reverse or turning pass from his centre. The centre's run simulates a path as if he is being forced to run across the field.

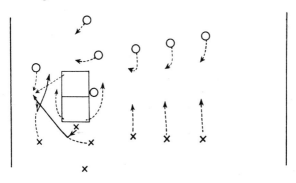

9. The fly-half runs to the blind side and accepts the scrum-half's pass as he runs across the base of the scrum. He runs wide and flat to draw the blind-side wing and wing-forward, and gives the ball to his own wing using the reverse pass. As in all these moves the wing must run with great determination, for a moment's hesitation might ruin the move.

147

The same tactic could be tried with the scrum-half breaking wide to the blind side instead of the fly-half.

Another variation is to use the full back as a decoy outside the wing.

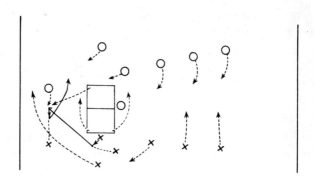

Cardiff v. Oxford University. S. B. Richards, Oxford forward comes away with the ball

French players in practice. The receiver is about to catch the ball well to his right so that it can be passed without delay in the next stride. Eyes on the ball and fingers well spread

17/Centre-threequarter

A CENTRE is essentially an attacking player. This thought must be uppermost and constantly in his mind and he must never cease to practise the arts of rugby required in good attacking play. His first duty is to make openings and provide his wing with opportunities to use his speed and skill to the fullest advantage, and unless he is able to do this several times during a game he is lacking in the essential requirements of a centre.

If the intention is to make play for the wing, the centre must first know the wing's needs and play his part accordingly before passing. In an orthodox passing movement no wing will want the ball too early when he has still some distance to cover before meeting the opposition. Not only will he have his own opposite number to defeat but the opposing outside-centre, seeing that his man has passed, will then move across to force the attacking wing outward, and the further out he goes the more time is given for the cover defence to move into position across field. Behind them will be the full-back. The wing's chances in this situation are very slight.

If the wing is given the ball too late he will either be crash-tackled as he receives it, or find himself with insufficient room to manœuvre.

The wing receives the ball too early

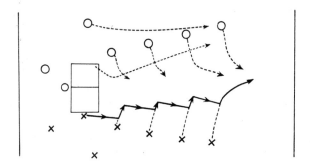

In an orthodox passing move to the wing the ball should be passed quickly to the outside-centre who must then try to give the ball to the wing so that he has only the full-back to beat. When he receives the ball the centre accelerates toward his man and straightens the line of attack to check the defence, and then veers outward in an attempt to round his man. On seeing this the opposing wing is liable to hesitate, thinking that his centre may be defeated. He will either turn inward to tackle the centre or momentarily slow down as a precaution. If he does either of those things, he is as good as beaten. The centre passes to the wing who accelerates outside his opponent and prepares to meet the challenge of the full-back. The centre has drawn two players, the opposing centre and wing, and created the half-opening for his own wing. No matter how well the centre does this the wing has his part to play, too, and unless he takes full advantage of the situation he cannot blame the centre for the service he gives. This is elementary centre play and the inside-centre will be expected to employ the same tactics to make the half-opening for the outside-centre. The logical progression from this move is for the centre to actually round his man and sprint through the gap between the centre and wing and run up to the full-back before passing. The wing will then have an unopposed run to the line.

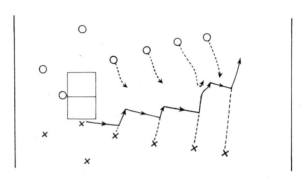

The vital phase of the centre's play is to straighten his run, and this he must do whenever he intends to beat a man on the outside, unless, of course, he is very much faster than his opponent or if the latter has been slow in coming up in defence.

Straight running must feature prominently in a centre's methods of attack and it must be resolute and fast. When watching some players it is sometimes felt that their running is half-hearted. They seem to hold themselves back and the running lacks confidence, power and determination. If a centre decides to make a break on his own by using straight running then he must go for, and through, the gap, with all the speed and determination he can muster. He must strongly resist the temptation to run across the field in three-quarter movements and remedy the weakness of allowing himself to be shepherded in that direction by the defence. Running diagonally is sometimes inevitable and the centre must take the slightest opportunity to change his direction and run straight and hard, unless the diagonal run is of some definite purpose such as luring the defence across to that side and not because the defence compels him to do so.

Speed and controlled running are vital basic needs in a centre and he must master all the arts of evasion. Ideally he should be as fast as a wing and possess extraordinary acceleration. A centre will often find that to come to a sudden stop is the best way of avoiding a tackle, and unless he has the ability to regain top speed in a few strides he may be caught by another defender and the opportunity will have been lost.

He must always be on the alert to take advantage of the slightest opportunity to defeat the defence, and he must have the ability and anticipation to follow the fly-half in attack no matter how elusive and unorthodox the latter may be. The unorthodox player's extraordinary skill and individuality in attack is often wrongly criticised for his lone and sometimes fruitless runs, when it is the rest of the team, and particularly the middle backs, who should be criticised for their failure to back up effectively.

A centre must be an expert handler of the ball, having mastered all forms of passing and dummying and be able to take and give a pass in one movement without delaying the ball's progress. He must never pass to a player who is not better placed in the attack than himself, and he must always pass if the chances of scoring are improved by his doing so.

He should decide what form of individual attack he intends to use before receiving the ball and he must clearly inform his colleagues of his intention so that they can be prepared to back him up, and at the same time he must be prepared to abandon this move at the last moment and use something else should the situation warrant it. For example, he might decide to take a short pass from the fly-half and try the straight burst inside his man, but if his opponent is slow up in defence the centre's obvious move now is to veer outward and accelerate through the gap between the two centres.

The centre must be good in defence as well as in attack. His tackling must always be sure and hard. When moving up in defence he must keep in alignment with the rest of the 'threes' and keep just inside his opponent's line of approach to force the movement outward to the touch-line.

Even in defence the centre must be thinking of attacks or counter-attacks. Very often miskicks by the opponents are fielded by the full-back in positions which favour counter-attacks, and because the full-back lacks support he feels disinclined to start one. This is where the centre helps. During the kick (by the opponents) he should automatically drop back level with the full-back, and if the opportunity is present he is on hand to give the full-back the necessary encouragement and support to start an attack.

Tactics in Attack

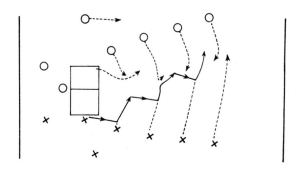

1. The inside-centre makes a half-opening for the outside-centre by half drawing the opposing outside-centre.

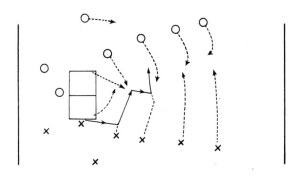

2. The inside-centre breaks through by using the straight burst. It is important that the fly-half runs well up to his man almost to the point of being tackled before he passes to the centre. The centre must change the direction of his run before receiving and run with great determination. The open-side wing-forward must be in a position to back up.

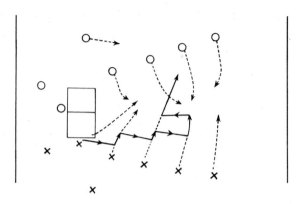

3. The ball is passed quickly to the outside-centre thus drawing the defending backs across the field. The outside-centre retains the ball long enough to draw the opposing inside-centre toward him, and then passes inside to his own inside-centre who runs straight and hard. He should be backed up by the fly-half and open-side wing-forward.

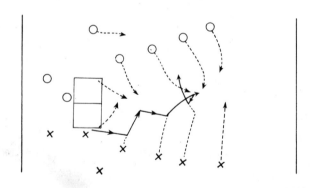

4. The outside-centre cuts inside and behind the inside-centre and takes the reverse, inside, or turning

pass. The outside-centre must first run along with the inside-centre to conceal his move until the last moment.

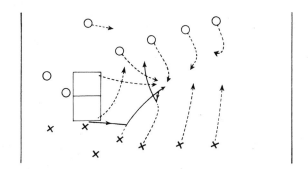

5. The inside-centre cuts inside and behind the fly-half to take the reverse pass.

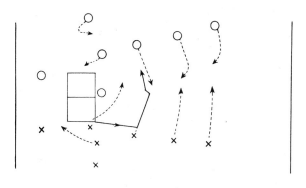

6. The fly-half runs to the blind side calling for the ball and acts as a decoy to lure the defence to that side. The scrum-half passes directly to the inside-centre who defeats his opposite number with a side-step. The open-side wing-forward backs up.

7. The fly-half runs wide and fast to draw the defence. The inside-centre cuts inside behind the fly-half

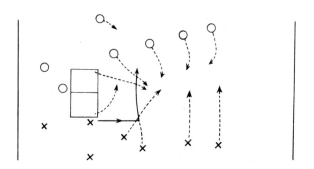

and takes the scrum-half's pass. This move must be tried when the fly-half is very closely watched by a fast-breaking wing-forward.

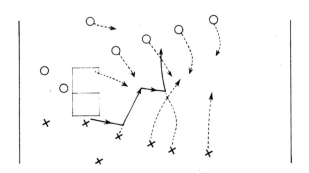

8. The fly-half runs to draw the defence. The inside-centre runs parallel with the fly-half to attract his opposite number, and the outside-centre cuts inward behind the inside-centre to take the fly-half's pass.

9. The fly-half runs to the left of the scrum calling for the ball and acts as a decoy. The left-centre moves across behind the fly-half to the right of the scrum and receives the ball from the scrum-half. The left-centre

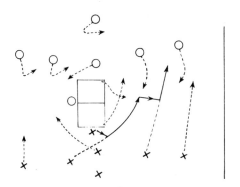

either draws the opposing left-centre or makes a clear break-through.

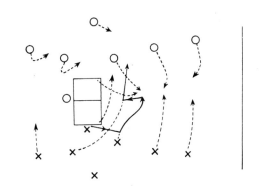

10. The fly-half takes the ball on the open side and runs diagonally for a short distance to draw the defence outward, and then straightens his run a few paces before he passes inward to the blind-side centre who has moved across to the open side between the fly-half and the scrum.

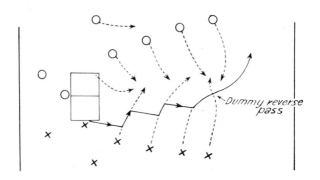

11. The outside-centre and wing go through the 'scissors' movement but the centre has realised that the opponents have anticipated the move. He therefore dummies the reverse pass, retains the ball, and continues outward round the opposing wing. The in-moving wing calls for the ball to attract the opposition if the move is prearranged.

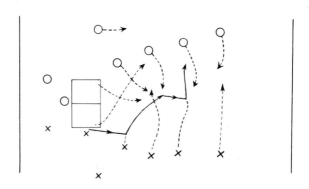

12. After receiving the scrum-half's pass, the fly-half runs wide; the inside-centre cuts inside and behind the

fly-half to employ the dummy 'scissors' movement. The fly-half performs the dummy reverse pass to the inside-centre and then passes the ball outward to the outside-centre who runs hard and straight between the two opposing centres.

18 / Fly-half

Much of what has been written about the centres applies also to the fly-half. He must be a complete tactician and possess the ability to put his knowledge into practice. His responsibility to the rest of the team is somewhat greater than that of the centre because he is in the vital position of being able to dictate the general tactics of the threequarter line. If he fails as an attacker, or serves merely as a link between the scrum-half and the centres, then the threequarters are not likely to succeed. The fly-half must assume the duty of being the instigator of most of the attacks, not only by making clear-cut openings on his own but by giving speed and direction to the attacks generally, to make half-openings for the centres by drawing opponents, and by acting as a decoy to lure the opponents away from the main point of attack. His general play must be such that he is a constant source of annoyance and worry to the opposition.

He must decide what form of attack he intends to take before he receives the ball and he must inform the centres of his intention, though he should be ready with an alternative tactic should the need for it arise. For instance, should he decide to make a half-opening for his centre and sees that the defence is so out of position that he could break through himself, then he should do so. On the other hand, if, after deciding to make a clear-cut opening, he finds that he cannot, he should not then pass to his centre, unless the centre, having anticipated his failure, calls for the ball.

Many young fly-halves fail because they cannot get out of the habit of standing and taking the ball with the body turned toward the scrum-half and, having taken the ball facing the wrong way, they abandon the thought of attack. The inevitable kick to touch over the scrum follows. When standing ready to receive the ball the fly-half should have feet and body facing the direction of the attack and only the head should be turned toward the scrum-half. He should be so placed that he takes the ball as he accelerates into top speed.

Another mistake many fly-halves make is to stand too deep before an attack. When the fly-half stands deep, the threequarters feel compelled to do the same to keep behind the man with the ball. A threequarter-line standing deep is considered to be on the attack, and a line which stands flat, or shallow, is assumed to be defending. This is not strictly true in modern rugby. Many of the unorthodox moves and those involving the extra man in attack are best executed when the three-quarters stand fairly flat, and when quick passing and not running speed is the best means of leading up to the break-through.

Standing deep in attack is often a mistake and a sign of weakness in the attacking ability of the fly-half and threequarters. They do so because they need the room and time for passing, and the distance to build up speed. It means that the attackers have further to run before they cross the advantage line (an imaginary line running through the middle of the scrum and line-out and parallel with the goal lines) and begin to gain ground—usually they never reach it because the defenders have crossed it first—and it gives the defenders more time to place themselves in good defensive positions. Furthermore, the direction of the attack is usually more across the field, particularly in a movement following a line-out. Standing shallower places the attacker near to the advantage line and gives the forward defenders less time to move into position. There is little to be gained by standing deep and it is a waste of energy, because players run further than they need. The important qualities to aim for are good acceleration to reach the necessary speed in a short distance, and the ability to pass very quickly. It is not suggested that all attacks should start from a shallow position, but the point is made that most attacks are started from a too-deep position.

Fly-halves and threequarters find a shallow defence a problem. This defence is in fact difficult to defeat in orthodox play and, if use of the short punt fails to drive them to deeper positions, then unorthodox tactics must be employed, and the obvious way is to increase the number of attackers by introducing the extra man. It is assumed that each defender has an opposite number to mark, and if the defenders fulfil their duties correctly they cannot mark their own men and occupy the spaces at the same time. The attackers should stand reasonably close to the advantage line to encourage the defenders to approach quickly and straight, and the extra man brought in either between the fly-half and the scrum or first centre, or between the centres. Split-second timing by the passers and the extra man is essential, and the latter should delay his entry into the move until the last second when all the defenders are occupied marking their own men. Once a player breaks through a shallow defence the result is obvious. The fly-half must be an exponent of the short punt ahead, the long diagonal kicks to the wings, and the drop kick, but he should use them with discretion and not rely on them as his main source of attack.

The fly-half's role in attack is not an easy one, therefore he must possess exceptional acceleration, speed, and evading skill, if he is to contribute fully to his team's attack. He must never cease trying to evolve new ideas to outwit the defence. Not only will he require the speed to outflank the fast-breaking wing-forward, but he must also know how to take advantage of this fast break by attacking on the inside. A fast-breaking wing-forward frequently leaves a wide gap between himself and the scrum, and unless the fly-half sees and takes advantage of it either by straight running, inside break, or bringing in the extra man, many good opportunities will be lost.

He is expected to take a full part in defence, and by virtue of his position fairly near the scrum and line out he may occasionally be expected to tackle forwards in full cry for the try line. To prevent a score, the fly-half will be required to use the head-on or smother tackle which drives the opponent backwards away from the line. Once his opposite number has passed on the ball in attack, the fly-half must then cover across the field behind his threequarters always keeping just inside the ball as it moves from player to player towards the wing.

Tactics in Attack

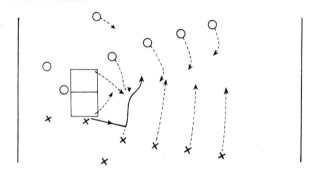

1. The fly-half takes the scrum-half's pass and runs straight toward his opponents. He then swerves outward to make the opening on the outside.

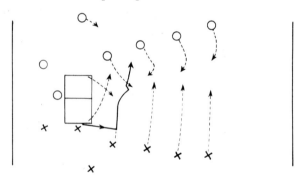

2. The fly-half runs straight to check the wing-forward, and then swerves outward for a short distance until he is in the right position to side-step inside the

opposing fly-half who has relied on the wing-forward to
stop the inside break-through.

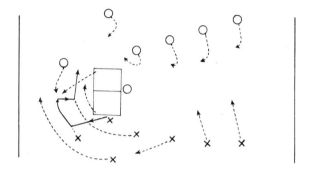

3. The scrum-half passes to the blind-side wing, who
draws his opposite number and the blind-side wing-
forward. In the meantime the fly-half runs across to the
blind side between the wing and the scrum and takes
the wing's inside pass. Both the blind-side wing-forward
and the full-back join in the move to back up.

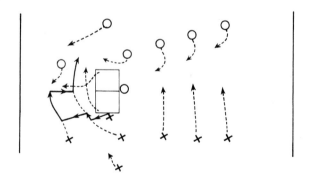

4. A variation of the previous move. The fly-half runs to the blind side to take the scrum-half's pass and almost immediately passes to the wing. All the defenders automatically run to cover the wing, and once they are drawn the wing returns the ball to the fly-half to break through.

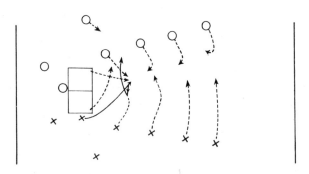

5. The scrum-half runs wide. The fly-half cuts inside behind the scrum-half and takes the reverse pass.

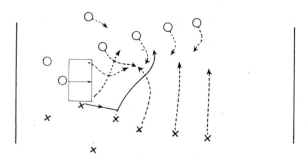

6. The inside centre moves for the 'scissors' movements with the fly-half, but the fly-half dummies the reverse pass and breaks through between the two opposing centres.

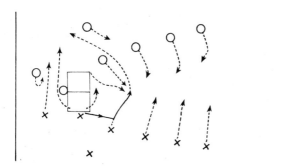

7. The fly-half runs with the ball to the open side and then cross kicks to the blind side for the blind-side wing and wing-forward.

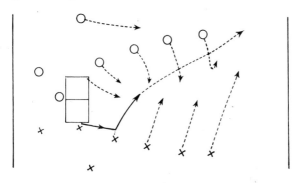

8. The fly-half uses the long diagonal kick for the open-side wing.

The tackle that failed

Neath scrum-half, R. Richards, gets a kick in after receiving the ball from a scrum

19 / The Scrum-half

MANY rugby followers believe that the scrum-half has taken over from the fly-half the role of being the chief instigator of most of the attacks from the scrum and line-out. Whether this is true or not the scrum-half's contribution in giving variety and speed to the attacks is very important.

His first duty is to send out a long, accurate, and rapid pass to the fly-half immediately he takes the ball into his hands. A second's delay after picking up the ball may mean the difference between the success and failure of the ensuing attack. The action of picking up the ball and passing is one whole movement. No time should be wasted in winding up for the pass and looking to see where the fly-half is. A good scrum-half knows by instinct where to pass the ball, and through constant practice with his partner he will know when the fly-half starts his run and how fast he travels.

He must master all forms of passing and on occasions be able to pass to one of the centres as a variation, and to gain an extra few seconds in attack. But if passing from the scrum and line-out is the scrum-half's only form of play he will be giving the opposing wing-forwards the opportunity to concentrate wholeheartedly on the fly-half. He must avoid this situation from developing by probing here and there around the scrum, and darting away on his own, or by making use of his own wing-forwards as attackers so that the opposing back-row forwards are compelled to delay their covering defence and are constantly kept in a state of uncertainty. This gives the fly-half those extra vital seconds in attack when the ball is sent to him. Should the scrum-half decide to run with the ball he must run straight and not across the field in his endeavour to make a successful break-through or, an opening for one of his colleagues. It is of no use running a few paces and then passing to the fly-half when an opening no longer exists. By this time the fly-half will be closely marked and will most certainly be tackled in possession. The scrum-half must take full advantage of any gap left near the scrum by a fast-breaking wing-forward.

The scrum-half must have a variety of tactics at his finger-tips so that he can combine in surprise attacks with the fly-half, the first centre, the blind-side wing, both wing-forwards, and the full-back when the latter joins as an extra man near the scrum.

He must be quick and agile in everything he does and be here, there, and everywhere. Wherever the play is the scrum-half is expected to be near by to snap up the loose ball, to start a new attack, and lend a hand generally in attack and defence.

He should be able to punt accurately with either foot.

The scrum-half must be courageous in defence generally. When the opponents gain possession in the scrum many scrum-halves follow their opposite numbers round it and endeavour to tackle them in possession while in the process of gathering the ball. Some of the great scrum-halves do this only if the heeling is slow and if the opposing scrum-half takes longer than normal to gather and pass the ball. Against good scrum-halves they prefer to double back round the scrum and cover across the field behind the threequarters leaving the blind-side wing-forward to keep his eye on the opposing scrum-half until he passes to his fly-half. This seems the logical thing to do for it adds depth to the defence, and the scrum-half is still well placed to counter a break-through by the attacking scrum-half on the open side of the scrum.

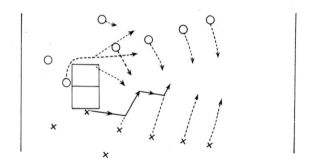

The defending scrum-half covers behind the three-quarters in an orthodox passing movement.

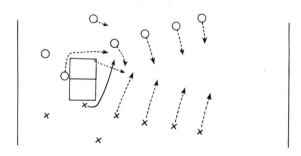

The defending scrum-half is in position to defend against a break through by the attacking scrum-half on the open side.

The scrum-half should drop back to take the full-back's place should the latter join in a three-quarter movement. He will then be in position to cover a possible interception or kick through by the opponents.

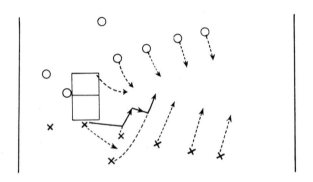

Tactics in Attack in which the Scrum-half Plays a Leading Role

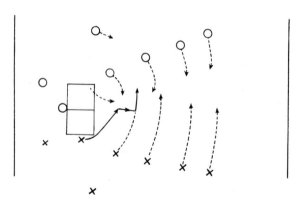

1. The scrum-half breaks wide on the open side to draw the opposing fly-half and wing-forward and makes a half-opening for his fly-half.

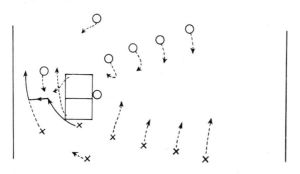

2. The scrum-half breaks wide on the blind side to draw the opposing wing and wing-forward and makes an opening for his blind-side wing. The fly-half attracts attention on the open side by running that way and calling for the ball.

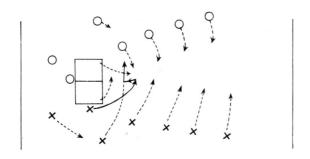

3. The scrum-half breaks wide on the open side to draw the defence outward and then passes inside to the full-back.

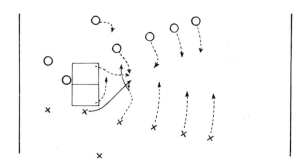

4. The scrum-half runs wide on the open side, the fly-half cuts inside to employ the 'scissors' movement, and takes a reverse pass from the scrum-half. The fly-half should run outside and parallel with the scrum-half until the latter has completely drawn the wing-forward, before cutting inward.

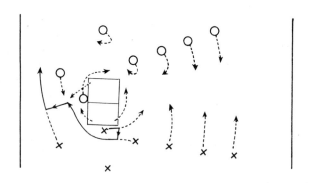

5. The scrum-half runs a few paces to the open side before passing to the fly-half, who runs to the blind side, and continues to run to the open after passing as a decoy. When challenged the fly-half passes to the blind-side wing.

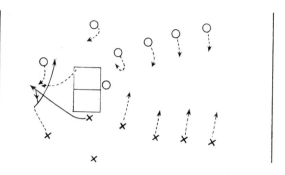

6. The scrum-half runs wide on the blind side to draw the wing-forward and wing and gives a reverse pass to his own wing who cuts inside. Should the defence anticipate the 'scissors' movement the scrum-half should retain the ball and continue on the outside to make a break-through on his own.

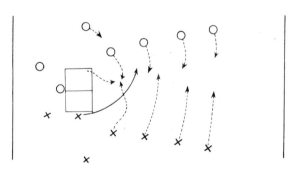

7. Here the halves combine to employ the dummy 'scissors' movement. The scrum-half retains the ball after performing the dummy reverse pass and breaks through between the opposing fly-half and the inside-centre. Should the inside centre challenge the scrum-half the latter would then pass to his own inside-centre.

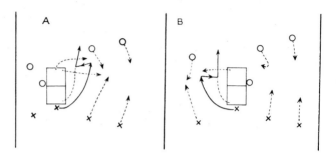

8. In (a) the defending open-side wing-forward has broken early toward the fly-half, giving the scrum-half the opportunity to break through between him and the scrum. When challenged by No. 8 the scrum-half passes inside to his own open-side wing-forward.

(b) The scrum half breaks to the blind side and when challenged by the defending wing-forward he passes inside to his blind-side wing-forward.

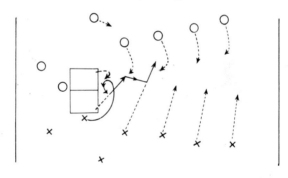

9. This is a variation of tactic 8. Instead of running wide the scrum-half runs as far as he can very close to the scrum to keep the defence in, and after running well up to the wing-forward he turns inward in a semi-circle, to present his back to the defence, and

passes to the open-side wing-forward who runs for an opening or to draw the fly-half and pass. The same move can be used on the blind side, using the wing-forward on that side of the scrum.

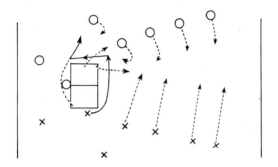

10. The defending open-side wing-forward breaks early. The scrum-half breaks through on the open side and passes to the blind-side wing-forward.

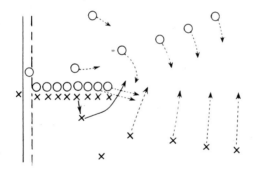

11. The attacking scrum-half runs a few paces and dummies a pass to the fly-half. Both defending wing-forwards run to cover the fly-half and leave the way open for the scrum-half.

20 / Forwards

THE first duty of the forwards is to gain possession of the ball from the tight and loose scrums and line-out, and give it to the backs as often and as speedily as possible. To do this effectively it is essential that the forwards play as a unit and not as eight individuals, so that every phase of play is undertaken with complete understanding, purpose and precision. A good pack leader is essential. He must be a player outstanding in the ability to assess a situation quickly and provide the appropriate tactic. He must be a stickler for discipline in training and practice drills, and must drive his forwards into giving one hundred per cent effort in the games, yet he must be prepared to encourage and give praise when it is due.

The forward's duties do not end after gaining possession of the ball. He will be expected to back up intelligently in attack and be prepared to join the handling movements and run with real speed and determination. In the past, most forwards have been considered poor handlers of the ball and the majority have not felt the need to practise handling like the backs. Yet in the line-out and at close quarters they are expected to catch and pass the ball in most difficult conditions, far more difficult than handling in a three-quarter movement when there is more time and space in which to do it. Little wonder then that scrum and fly-halves are so often tackled in possession, that many line-outs resolve into loose scrummages and very often a stoppage, and that so few tactics can be tried by the forwards from the line-outs. The lack of handling ability is the one great limiting factor in tactical play in rugby.

The new laws concerning the method of playing the ball after a tackle and taking a penalty kick by the tap-back method are incentives to forwards to improve their handling. Forwards must concentrate more on handling, especially short and close inter-passing as a pack, and picking up and passing while on the move. The tap-back penalty kick gives forwards ample opportunity to use their weight and power to break through by straight running and short inter-passing between themselves. Good handling at close quarters is essential, and this should be practised religiously in the training sessions. At first it should be practised against seven or eight players standing still, or posts about 5 feet high, arranged in a casual and fairly deep group.

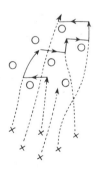

The player with the ball should aim to run through a gap between two players or posts, and immediately after going through he passes to right or left to the next attacker, who does the same, and so on until the ball has been carried and passed through the stationary group.

As handling at close quarters improves, the activity can be speeded up and the defenders offer 'token' opposition by leaning or taking a short step toward the player with the ball as if to tackle him low. Later, when tackling is used, the player with the ball should ensure that the arms are kept free so that he can pass from the tackle and while falling in order to keep the movement going. Another good practice is to play modified rugby (see Passing Practices) across the field in the 25-yards area.

From the tap-back penalty, the forward should be prepared to start an attack to one side of the field to draw the defending forwards across, and have the ability to quickly switch it in the opposite direction for the backs to attack on the other side.

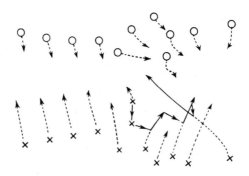

With study and practice the forwards could evolve and perfect even more complex tactics from such a position.

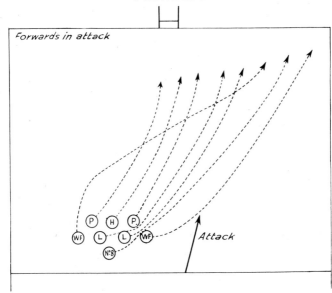

Forwards in attack

P H P

WF L L WF

N°8

Attack

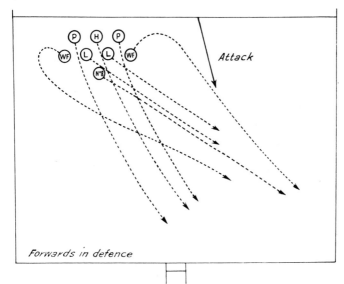

Attack

P H P

WF L L WF

N°8

Forwards in defence

Each forward has his own basic path to follow in both attack and defence as shown in the diagrams, but it must be remembered that they serve only as a general guide and the forward should be prepared to deviate from them to be where his presence is best served at any given moment. For example, the front-row forwards are recommended to run deep in defence, roughly down the centre of the field toward the goal posts, but if the need arises for one of them to race to the corner flag to cut off an attacking wing, and perhaps, bring off a try-saving tackle, he should obviously do so.

Wing-forwards—in Defence

The first duty of the wing-forward is to ensure that a break-through does not materialise close to the scrum either by the opposing scrum-half, by the combined play of the scrum-half and a wing-forward who is being used as an attacker, or by any other player who joins the attack as an extra man near the scrum, e.g. blind-side wing or full-back. This applies to both open-side and blind-side wing-forwards.

If an attack develops on the open side, the open-side wing-forward, after seeing that the scrum-half has passed the ball to his fly-half, runs diagonally outward to harass the fly-half, prevent an inside break-through and, if possible, tackle him in possession, or force him to run across the field. Should the fly-half pass the ball, the wing-forward then continues outward to harass the centres and wing, but if he is being left behind by the speed of the attack he must cover toward the corner flag and try to cut off the attack before it reaches the try line.

When the scrum-half puts the ball into the scrum on the open side, the open-side wing-forward may then run straight toward the fly-half because the opposing scrum-half is more likely to try a break through on the blind side and the defending scrum-half is in position to deal with him if he tries on the open side. Even so, the open-side wing forward should not do this unless he has delegated to his No. 8 the responsibility of looking after the opposing scrum-half.

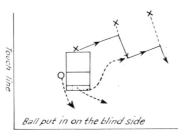

Ball put in on the blind side

(a)   Ball put in on blind side

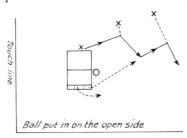

Ball put in on the open side

(b)   Ball put in on open side

The blind-side wing-forward breaks diagonally to that side of the scrum to cover the scrum-half and the fly-half should either, or both, try a move on the blind side. If the attack by the opposition goes to the open side he turns to run behind the scrum to cover across the field. If his own scrum-half doubles back round the scrum to cover defensively across the field behind the backs, the blind-side wing-forward tries to tackle the attacking scrum-half in the process of gathering the ball before passing.

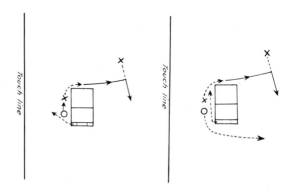

From the Kick-off

The blind-side wing-forward stands deep near the touch-line while the open-side wing-forward stands just beyond the centre line between the two sets of goal posts to prevent a surprise attack to that side (see diagram).

186

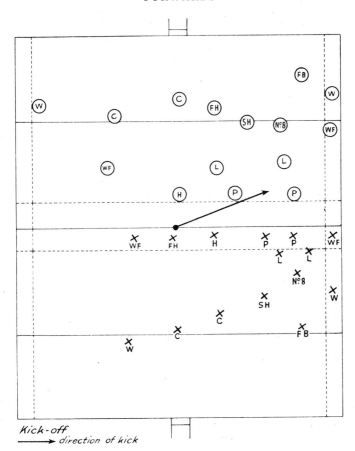

Kick-off
——→ *direction of kick*

From the Line-out

Usually the wing-forwards stand at the back of the line-out and must first ensure that the scrum-half cannot make a break. Their next target is the opposing fly-half who receives the scrum-half's pass. Should the fly-half pass in turn the defensive covering is as from a scrum, or one wing-forward goes directly for the fly-half while the other waits to cover a possible break by the scrum-half.

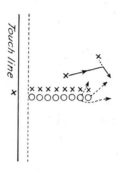

Both wing-forwards should not go directly to the fly-half before the scrum-half passes, nor should they take the 'dummy' from the scrum-half and leave a gap at the back of the line.

In Attack

To back up an attack on the open side, the open-side wing-forward takes up a position inside and just behind the player with the ball. He must be ready for an inside pass from any one of the backs and to pounce on a loose ball and continue that attack should it temporarily break down because of a dropped pass, but he must be sure not to get in the way or impede the backs in any way.

The blind-side wing-forward breaks to that side and runs forward round the scrum and makes for a point inside and just behind No. 8 and the open-side wing-forward. On his way he must be ready for a cross-kick into the centre of the field.

Both wing-forwards must combine with the scrum-half in attacks round the scrum as described in the scrum-half tactics.

No. 8—in Defence

No. 8 breaks to the side of the attack, first to cover a possible break-through by the scrum-half and then to cover across the field behind the backs toward the corner flag. He is more likely than the open-side wing-forward to reach the touch-line first to tackle the wing or to gather a possible diagonal kick by the fly-half toward the corner flag, for his wing. He must be prepared to cover a possible mistake by the full-back should the attack take the form of a kick ahead towards the latter.

From the Line out

No. 8 may be one of the line-out 'specialists' and therefore may not be in a position to harass the half-backs, in which case, when the attack starts, he disengages himself from the line-out and corner flags.

From the Kick-off

He stands deep, about 8–10 yards in from the touch-line ready to catch the ball and start an attack should the ball be kicked to him. The only tactic most forwards have when they receive the ball in such circumstances is to kick it to touch. They give up possession immediately after gaining it. *The best policy is to keep possession and attack*. Should another player catch the ball near the touch-line, No. 8 must be prepared to take a pass and be the link in the attack between the catcher and the three-quarters.

In Attack

No. 8 breaks to the side of the attack to back up inside and just behind the open-side wing-forward. He too must be prepared to cover a mistake by the backs and pick up a loose ball at speed and continue the attack.

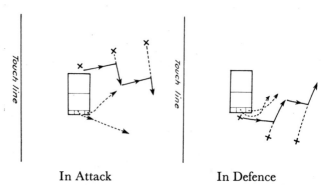

In Attack   In Defence

Second Row Forwards (Locks) In Defence from the Scrums

These forwards break to the side of the attack and run back fairly deep. Their first aim is counter a pos-

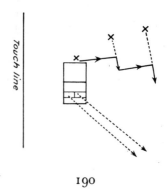

sible inside break-through by the centres and then cover across the field toward the corner flag. They will have little chance to stop a break-through by the fly-half but may be in time to foil the centres.

From the Line out

The second-row men are usually the two main line-out specialists. Once this duty ends they corner flag.

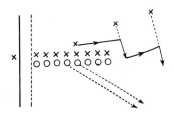

In Attack—from the Scrums

Both forwards break clear to the side of the attack and back up inside and a little behind the blind-side wing-forward, but should the latter be delayed en route they will back up inside No. 8.

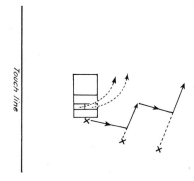

Front-row Forwards—in Defence from the Scrums

All three break as quickly as they can from the scrum and run back roughly down the centre of the field towards the goal posts, and must be prepared for a cross-kick as well as a break-through down the middle by the opposing middle backs. Generally they will have little chance of getting to the touch-line to cut off an attack, but there may be occasions when this is possible. It depends on how quickly the scrum breaks up and on how fast these forwards can run.

From the Line out

Corner flag on the side of the attack.

In Attack—from the Scrums

Once clear of the scrum they should run roughly up the centre of the field in the line of the attack, backing up inside and behind the second row forwards. When the front row forwards are in position all the forwards should be in a diagonal line formation across the field each a little behind the player next to him nearest the ball.